The Best of

GOTTLIEB'S
BOTTOM LINE

The Best of
GOTTLIEB'S
BOTTOM LINE

A Practical Profit Guide for Today's Foodservice Operator

by Leon Gottlieb

Lebhar-Friedman Books
Chain Store Publishing Corp.
A Subsidiary of Lebhar-Friedman, Inc.
New York

5 4 3 2 1

Library of Congress Cataloging in Publication Data
Gottlieb, Leon, 1927-
    The best of Gottlieb's bottom line.

    1.   Restaurant management.   I.   Title.
TX911.3.M27G68   647'.95'068   80-16535
ISBN 0-912016-39-6

CONTENTS

FOREWORD

The nineteen eighties promise to be a period of maximum economic pressure on foodservice operators—chains and independents alike. Inflationary spirals, a tightening of credit, and a lack of enough well-trained people to staff the expanding number of foodservice operations pose severe challenges.

But opportunities for success in the restaurant field are unparalleled in terms of reaching the goals of personal career development and financial rewards. Those who can manage their businesses professionally and motivate their employees to excel will survive and prosper no matter how tough the conditions. Others are likely to drop out of the running.

With so much at stake, a book on the basics of achieving these goals was urgently needed. This is why Leon Gottlieb decided to compile the best of his *Gottlieb's Bottom Line* monthly newsletters into this highly readable, tight package containing the leading principles. These principles will be especially crucial in the eighties.

This collection gives valuable pointers to restaurant managers and executives on the real basics of the business: motivating personnel, setting management policies, hiring and training, sales promotion and advertising, and cost savings and security.

In a word, it provides common sense answers to the daily and long-range problems faced by almost every foodservice operator. It is *must* reading for anyone who wants to gain that extra edge on the competition and be one of the prospering survivors.

Charles Bernstein
Editor
Nation's Restaurant News
Lebhar-Friedman, Inc.

ACKNOWLEDGMENTS

I would like to thank my fine professional associates, Robert Tallent and Lawrence Toolin. I am grateful as well to my clients, who allowed me to make reference to both positive and negative situations, and to the newsletter subscribers, who made *Gottlieb's Bottom Line* newsletter possible and successful. I would also like to thank my son Mark and my daughter Diane for their work. And finally, I want to thank my terrific wife Madaline, for putting up with my note taking wherever we were, in restaurants and hotels. To all, my sincere appreciation.

INTRODUCTION

Gottlieb's Bottom Line newsletter was born in 1974 out of what I felt was a need for a straight-from-the-shoulder communication device aimed at owners, executives, all levels of management, and, most specifically, at unit-level managers of foodservice and hospitality organizations. Fortunately, a sufficient number of subscribers agreed with this approach, and supported the newsletter with their money, suggestions, and compliments.

Every article, every problem, solution, and recommendation presented in the newsletter and collected in this volume comes from the real world of foodservice. The items here are equally applicable to fast fooders, family coffee shops, and dinnerhouses of every type, whether independent or chain.

My associates and I have tried to remain true to our philosophy of the importance of the 3 Ps: Patrons, Personnel, and Profits. We have attempted to recommend systems and procedures based upon whatever would be good for the 3 Ps. We felt that if we could accomplish this, our readers, similarly, would reap the benefits. They would be able to avoid many of the pitfalls that we either observed or experienced as executives who worked our way up from the bottom to the top of the national chains.

It is my hope that you, my valued customers and readers, will get the most from each section. The hundreds of problem/solution examples presented here are examples of the problems that daily confront us in this, the toughest of businesses. As you read through this collection I hope you will come to understand that your own problems are not as unique as you once thought; others have experienced similar situations and solved them.

This is your handbook—your own management manual of operations. Enjoy it and use it.

Leon Gottlieb
Tarzana, California
1980

HIRING

YOUR EMPLOYEES

*All restaurant crews
have willing people:
those willing to work
and those willing to let them.*

1

HIRING YOUR EMPLOYEES

You have entered into a contract the very moment you say, "Yes, you are hired" and your prospective employee says, "Thank you, I will work for you."

True, your relationship may not be documented in writing, although many have used the employment agreement that you will find in the appendix to reinforce your pact. But make no mistake about it, you do have an agreement. It is your responsibility to explain fully what you as the employer will do for the employee and what you expect the employee to do for you. The better you communicate, the greater will be your chances for a good working relationship that can lead to trust, respect, pride, and dedication to your principles and objectives.

On-the-job-training commences the very minute you both agree to work together. Your new employee will be on Cloud Nine the moment you say he or she is hired. It is up to you to keep your people "up" and motivated. This section will give you many new slants on this important first meeting.

Mob Scene

Two's company; three's a crowd. What would you call a group of several hundred? It could be considered a mob if it were unruly. Or it could be a waiting line of prospective employees who have answered your help wanted advertisements. Recently, job opportunities have attracted unusually large numbers of persons. It is not unusual to see ten-fold numbers show up for a few job openings.

Prospective employees are also potential customers for most operations.

Several dozen applicants may represent hundreds of family members and friends. How they are treated becomes a job for a public relations expert as much as a job for a personnel manager.

☑ *B/L Recommends:* Do not brush off the unemployed so quickly. Determine to capitalize on their availability and interest in your establishment. One company we worked with as it was opening one or two operations per month faced this problem and handled it beautifully. They realized the tremendous potential value and goodwill of their new applicants. Together we created special coffee and soft drink chits. We distributed them along with price-off discount tickets to all who applied. Every person was given a complete, straightforward interview. Qualified individuals were hired or told they would be called in the event of any openings. All applicants were sent a thank you letter signed by the local manager. Reaction, as you can imagine, was extremely positive. For weeks following each new opening customers would remark how nicely and courteously they, their relatives, or friends were treated *before* the store opened. Word-of-mouth advertising can start well before you open your doors for business.

Head Start Program

"Attitude," by definition, is "a manner of acting, feeling or thinking that shows one's disposition, opinion, emotion, mood, etc." It is difficult for most managers to get an early opinion concerning the mental attitude of their new employees. Managers desperately *want new employees to care about and get involved* in their new work. They need every bit of information that can be gathered to help determine whether attitudes are good.

☑ *B/L Recommends:* Give prospective employees a souvenir menu, or copy of your regular one, to take home and *memorize*. When they have it memorized they can return for the balance of their employment interview and probable employment. One dinner house manager we are proud to work with uses this simple approach most effectively. He is able to determine if those who apply really do want a job badly enough to exert a little *effort up front before they are hired*. Obviously, those who do return exhibit a positive attitude and are eager and willing to learn and apply themselves to what is important to their employer. You can get a head start in helping your people acquire a positive attitude. This suggestion can be applied to every type of foodservice establishment.

Experienced Only Need Apply

Many managers attempt to use "experienced only" help wanted advertising in lieu of an effective training program. It is a practice that takes a heavy toll every year in accidents, lost job time, and labor turnover. True, the ad may attract someone that has worked in other restaurants. *The ad seldom, if ever, produces a worker that is experienced in the manager's own operation.* Every restaurant activity has a different operational profile. Equipment varies, as does its state of repair. Systems and procedures get altered in response to the desires of the person in charge. In the headlong rush to get a productive employee on the floor in the shortest amount of time, these facts are ignored. The new "experienced" employee is told to study the menu, and then spends perhaps a half shift being observed by the senior waitress or waiter on the floor, or the lead cook in the fry station. These employees are no doubt highly competent in their crafts, but their instructional skills almost never rate as high. The new "experienced" employees get a cursory walk through their work areas, an earful of gossip, and an admonition or two. After that, they are on their own.

☑ *B/L Recommends:* The sink-or-swim approach to the training of new employees is wasteful and, in some instances, nearly felonious. *Training is too important a subject to be left lying around in someone's head.* The minimum requirement for an elementary training program is a craft checklist. Whoever is in charge of instructing new employees should go over the checklist with the employee at the start and conclusion of whatever "break in" period is permitted by management.

Help Wanted—Second-Rate Only!

"If I kept every resume that comes in here, I'd need a warehouse for an office," said the operations director of a smallish regional coffee shop chain. Storage space was not the problem. The resume input for an entire year could have been accommodated in a shoe box. The operations director exaggerated the number of resumes received *because he looked on resumes as a threat to himself and his management clique.* So incoming resumes got dumped. When it was necessary to insert a new assistant manager into the chain of command, selection was based more on whim than individual merit and ability. The selection base narrowed as ambitious youngsters recognized the situation and left the company. While profits skidded, the company brass bravely chanted, "You just can't find good managers anymore."

☑ *B/L Recommends:* Whim and exigency are two forces that spawn second-rate management. *Equitable, clearly defined personnel policies help eradicate these influences.* Incoming resumes represent a potential company asset. They also serve as a barometer on how well a company is regarded within the foodservice community. It is a bad practice to treat resumes like junk mail.

Look for Night Owls After Dark

The jobs are classified the same, but the duties and responsibilities vary considerably. The night crew does more prep and cleaning work than the daytime force. They take care of a different customer element. There is less supervision, and therefore each position on the *night crew requires a more mature, responsible person*. Getting the right people for the night crew takes extra care.

☑ *B/L Recommends:* Hire night personnel *at night*, 10:00 p.m. for example. This will give you a better idea as to whether applicants pack the 5 P's necessary for night work: pep, pleasantness, punctuality, positiveness, and productivity. It will also show the job seeker that you are not loath to work at night. Many unsuitable candidates will eliminate themselves by calling and giving excuses for not showing up, or wander in late for the appointment.

Daytime interviewing for night jobs may be more convenient, but you are up against tougher odds in finding the right candidates.

Magicians or Witch-Doctors?

Some employment agencies and executive search firms (or head hunters, as they are often called) are real magicians when it comes to finding qualified candidates for you. They often make the right guy or gal appear just when you need them. But they also know how to make them disappear just as quickly. You know how hard it is to locate qualified people. It is not much easier for employment and search agencies. But they work at it all day long—every day. Their leads come from other people. They guard their sources most jealously.

This is one of the ways they operate: Firms plaster the industry in their area with resumes collected from applicants. Then, once they place persons in a position it is natural (so they believe) that they keep in touch with them. Their desire to "say hello" to your personnel, however, is really a wish to probe to determine who may be unhappy, who is thinking of leaving, and who is being terminated. It is in their interest to keep people churning about so that they can earn greater fees.

☑ *B/L Recommends:* Check the source of every resume you receive. Determine who prepared and sent it to you. Should you decide to deal with an employment agency or search firm, make it clear that you intend to pay only one fee for the filling of a position. Return all duplicate resumes to senders. Firms look to earn full or split fees whenever "their" applicants are successfully placed. More importantly, make sure these solicitors know you will not tolerate any recruiting advances made to your staff without your permission.

As food service consultants, we regularly receive dozens of calls each year from executive search firms who wish to offer us fees if we will suggest clients whom they can approach to place the prospects already on their rolls, as well as to find new ones who wish to make a change. The unethical ones are not magicians; they are scavengers. Be aware of their tricks. Save your money and personnel.

When Employees Hike, So Do Costs

The cost of recruiting employees has gone up. When the nation's unemployment rate is down, workers are scarce in many industries. Employers are turning to special training programs, the hiring of part-time workers, and added inducements to fill numerous job vacancies. *All this exacts a toll on the labor pool available to the restaurant industry.* In this situation hiring costs go up and job applicant qualifications and motivation go down. The manager who is used to churning through five or six workers a month is going to have operating problems.

☑ *B/L Recommends:* Keep track of recruiting costs. Ads, applicant interview time, employee entry expenses, and training costs all take a toll on profits. It is important to study the reasons for employee termination. Avoid repeating costly mistakes.

Ex-employees who move on to new jobs frequently attempt to proselytize your regular help. Beware of dropouts who come back to "just say hello to the gang." In a tight labor market, this can cause hiring expenses to snowball. Never allow names, addresses, or telephone numbers of your staff to be given out to anyone without your special okay.

College Recruiting

As the coach and team captain of your restaurant, it is your responsibility to recruit new players (employees) for your team. Most operations are always advertising or looking for new people.

☑ *B/L Recommends:* Line up a couple of high school or college *sororities and fraternities* (depending on the caliber of experience and age groups that you require). Offer them a work plan, wage scale, meal policies, and full- and part-time work schedules. Talk to the students to see how close you can come to meeting *their* needs. Write out your offer and post it on their club bulletin boards. Explain your interviewing practices. Then, treat them with extra courtesy and attention when they come in to apply.

Think When You Write Help-Wanted Ads!

A restaurant owner we know contacted a local junior college in the hope of finding a hostess for his operation. The school newspaper regularly publishes all job offers listed with the placement office. This is the way the position was listed:

RESTAURANT HOSTESS (City); Fri., Sat., Sun. & Mon. 2 p.m. to 10 p.m. Seat customers, serve water, take money, use cash register. Must be 21 yrs. or over, neat appearing, no experience necessary. Will train. $3.10/hr. to start.

Inspiring words? Do you think this low key ad will attract some sharp gal? Hardly.

☑ ***B/L Recommends:*** Make your offer an interesting and exciting one. Put yourself in the position of the applicant you want to attract. Try out this example:

HOSTESS (City); 4 evenings, 2-10 p.m. Well-known, popular restaurant. Meet people. Please be over 21 yrs. and neat in appearance, with/ without experience. Will train. Good basic wage plus fringe benefits, with increases based upon performance. Nice customers and people to work with.

Popping the Big Question

Checking applicant job references has always been difficult. But now restaurant managers are afraid that they'll have to steer clear of checking references altogether to avoid legal hassles. On the other hand, an operator who makes no attempt to check job references is taking a big risk. It's about as smart as stocking a store with empty fire extinguishers.

☑ ***B/L Recommends:*** *Keep checking those job references.* There is a way to get information from other managers without risking legal entanglements. When you contact an applicant's previous employer, limit your questions to confirming the work periods the applicant has supplied. Then, ask a simple, important question: *"Would you re-hire this person?"* The answer to that question will cover most of the things you need to know. Quite often the person you are calling will choose to amplify his answer with additional information. Or, if there is hesitation before answering your question, consider it as a warning that something is wrong somewhere.

A Nice Way to Lay It on the Line

He's with one of our client companies, so we can't pass along his name. Nonetheless, he's our candidate for Manager of the Month. He recently took over a high volume, good tip house. His biggest problem was poor staff discipline. *Instead of a crew, he had a collection of prima donnas.* Rather than get into "do it or else" skirmishing, he decided to try a more subtle approach first. He took the entire job application file to his initial meeting with all the employees. In the opening minutes of the agenda, he told the staff he was going to read off some names of current job applicants. If anybody knew these people, he said he would appreciate a recommendation. He explained that since he was new to the job, he really had no way of evaluating the applicants beyond what appeared on the form. Then he read off an impressively long string of names. He received hardly any recommendations. However, he has a very responsive staff these days; he hasn't had to refer to the job application file since the meeting.

☑ ***B/L Recommends:*** *Keep this tactic in mind.* It is a way to energize a crew that has become a little slack in accomplishing routine chores. It does not involve a lot of threats and aggravation. You don't have to wait to take over a new store. The recommendation idea can be announced as a new policy.

To Re-Hire or Not Re-Hire, That Is the Question

Generally, restaurant re-hire policies are dictated by circumstances and personalities. These are not good bases for decisions. The case against re-hires is that they frequently repeat the violations that led to the previous termination. There are morale factors to look at as well. *Returnees often regard themselves as enjoying privileged status.* They believe they know the politics, what's behind everything going on in the store. In an effort to establish a pseudo-seniority, they seek to impress co-workers with the idea they have special capabilities, things the boss cannot get along without. All this builds a very tense atmosphere. But the restaurant business is a notably pragmatic industry. Many managers are willing to accept future potential problems in exchange for an immediate solution to a labor shortage.

☑ *B/L Recommends:* A No Re-Hire Policy will avoid the aforementioned hazards. *It has to be rigidly enforced.* The instant a No Re-Hire Policy is breached, it becomes a Re-Hire Policy. When this happens, management leaves itself open to questions and criticism not only from employees, but from outside agencies and organizations as well. To make a No Re-Hire Policy work, employees have to be thoroughly aware of the rules when they are hired. It is a good idea to issue some of the rules when they are hired. It is a good idea to issue some periodic reminders. The policy will work as long as management is able to maintain its integrity.

Restaurant operations that do not wish to hew to such rigid employee practices can still avoid some of the difficulties presented by returnees. First, Re-Hire Policy conditions should be placed in writing. *There should be a stipulation that former employees must undergo retraining.* Note the emphasis on this point. As an owner or manager, it is your responsibility to put and keep returnees in their proper place. The regular employees will be watching to see how you handle the returnee situation. You will lose the respect of your crew if you allow returnees to goof off, get away with shortcuts, or violate the established chain of command. If the regulars get the impression there is some sort of double standard in effect regarding returnees, labor output will freeze up faster than anything your ice machine can accomplish. Make sure returnees understand you expect them to act like professionals in every sense of the word. Enforce this type of policy and you will greatly reduce your costs for aspirin as well as hidden labor expenses.

Help Wanted: Experienced Waiter or Waitress

Experience comes in many varying degrees. The person responding to your ad for help wanted may have worked a long time at his or her previous job, but *that does not necessarily mean he or she is completely competent*. The previous house may have tolerated table service and arm carries that can wreck a lot of food, dishes, and customer dispositions.

☑ *B/L Recommends:* As part of the hiring interview, set a series of dishes, cups and platters on a table. *Ask the applicant to pick them up*. This will give you an immediate reading on the degree of skill possessed by the applicant. From this you can decide whether he or she is going to need training on the floor with one of your senior serving personnel or if she or he is capable of handling a shift after minimum instructions.

Watch Out When They Start to Fade

Are you carrying any fading employees on the payroll? These are the ones that sort of fade off the labor schedule. *They need increasing amounts of time to meet sundry personal crises*. Sometimes, life works out that way. More often, we find it is an indication of lack of job interest.

☑ *B/L Recommends:* It does not pay to allow repeated absences from shifts. *Let your people know you are concerned, but also demanding*. Your house comes first. Employees would not be placed on the labor schedule if you did not need them.

Job Benefits Can Boomerang

New employees listen very carefully when told about coffee breaks, meal times and the other good features about the job. When it comes to less attractive aspects of the position, their attention and perception are not as keen. When management fails to meet the employee's expectations in the "goodies" department, job disenchantment ensues.

☑ *B/L Recommends:* Be very careful in explaining job benefits, *particularly the conditions under which the benefits are granted*. Some operators go to special lengths to "sell" an employee on the job benefits in the initial interview. The "dazzle effect" usually has a very short life span. The employee is unsold on his job the instant he or she feels a management promise has been bent or broken.

Effective Hiring

It would be no exaggeration to state that the major cause of terminations is poor hiring practices. Operators who bemoan the terrible rate of turnover existing in restaurants conveniently overlook the fact that, in too many cases, applicants who are totally unsuited to the needs of the industry are hired. In very short order, either the manager or the employee becomes dissatisfied, and another termination statistic is created.

In a business devoted to satisfying both the physical and emotional needs of its patrons, it would seem more than reasonable that management would devote at least as much time to the selection of personnel as to the selection of lettuce or tomatoes. To begin with, an applicant must have a desire to work under the special pressures of the foodservice industry. All applicants want jobs. Only a few really want jobs in food service. To hire someone lacking either the aptitude or the desire is to guarantee the waste of time, effort, and money, and ensure an inability on the part of the restaurant to satisfy its customers.

Under normal circumstances, the hiring process can be divided into four phases. These are: 1) Search, 2) Sort, 3) Cull, and 4) Indoctrinate. We will go into detail on each phase.

Search. Well-run restaurants have few personnel problems. There are always enough applicants on file, and turnover is minimal, because employees have security, both economic and psychological.

Less well-run restaurants are in a continual state of upheaval, and turnover is continuous.

One of the best sources of new employees is recommendations provided by present crew members. People throughout the industry are acquainted with other professionals, and they know who's looking.

Want ads are highly effective, although there are many operators who dispute this. The secret is in spending enough on a want ad to do the job economically. A miserly little two-line ad listing little more than a job title and phone number will attract no attention and no applicants.

An ad, listed alphabetically under "Man," will not be seen by a chef reading under the "C's."

A larger ad—one that can be seen—costs less in the long run, because it does what it is supposed to do.

Walk-in applicants are especially valuable because their approach is evidence of self-confidence. It isn't easy to walk into an interview cold. Those who do it well have special talents that anyone in the "people" business would be well advised to take advantage of. A waiter, waitress, hostess or cashier who handles a cold interview well has the ability to deal with the public in an outgoing—and profitable—manner.

The best employees are already on shift in a competitor's restaurant. These are people who do not remain out of work. They obviously satisfy their present employers.

It would hardly be honorable to suggest that personnel should be stolen from other restaurants, but there is nothing dishonorable about becoming well known, so that when a competitor's employee has decided to move along, your place is high up in consideration.

A frequently overlooked source of good employees is the current work force in the restaurant.

Present employees should be moved up into higher status vacancies. We are sick of hearing owners say, "He can't be a cook—he's a dishwasher." or, "She can't be a night manager—she's a waitress."

People are not limited to their present positions; they are capable of doing other things. No applicant should be hired *at all* unless he or she can demonstrate the ability to progress beyond the position for which you are interviewing.

Promotion from within is a standard procedure in industries that practice good personnel management policies.

Sort. In most operations, there are many more applications than there are vacancies. The process of deciding which applicant is best suited to the job is called sorting.

No one sorts with hundred-percent accuracy. Everybody hires applicants who should have not been considered, and everybody lets good professionals slip through their fingers.

There are some basic procedures that will aid in preventing mistakes in either direction:

1) Every applicant fills out an application on the premises. Those who take applications home seldom return them.
2) If the owner/manager is on the premises, and if humanly possible, he or she greets each applicant in person. If an interview cannot be conducted at that time, a definite appointment should be made for a more convenient time.
3) Appointments are obligations. It is not reasonable to expect an applicant to return for an appointment and be told that the manager forgot, and is not on the premises. No manager would hire an applicant who behaved with so little courtesy. It works both ways.
4) Notations should be made on the application concerning the applicant's strong and weak points. If a vacancy occurs at a later time, these notations will be vital in triggering the manager's memory of the applicant's qualifications.
5) When time permits, every applicant who has satisfactorily met the requirements for the position should be brought back for a second interview. Not only does a second interview confirm or disprove previously held opinions, it often brings out new factors. An applicant putting on an act would have trouble sustaining it through a second interview.
6) All applicants are to be treated with courtesy and consideration. It is not a crime to look for work, and there should be no reason to bully applicants.

Cull. When all the interviewing is over, and all the notations have been made, it is still necessary to select the one, best qualified applicant with the greatest aptitude.

Those who are not selected get culled.

One of the most effective means of culling is to get a second opinion. All first interviews should be conducted by the owner/manager. Second and subsequent interviews might be conducted by assistant managers, night managers, department supervisors, or well qualified fellow workers.

In general terms, the more opinions there are, the more likely a consensus will select the best person.

Those applicants who are not selected but who scored high in all levels of the selection process are kept on file for future vacancies. No one can predict when the next vacancy will occur.

Second-best applicants become first-best the second time around.

Units operating as part of a chain might pass along second-best applicants to other units in the community.

Indoctrination. The terms "indoctrination" and "training" are frequently used interchangeably. They are not necessarily interchangeable. Indoctrination takes place before training. It is the process of making the new employee feel at home and comfortable. It is a part of the process of bringing the new employee into the team.

Training is more effective if there has been good indoctrination.

When all the interviews are finished; when all the questions have been answered; when all the references have been checked, the final step is the owner/manager saying, "We'd like you to come work with us, and we want to make sure that this is the kind of work you're willing to do."

At that time, the applicant-employee is shown the work area. He or she sees other employees performing the jobs he or she will be expected to do. The applicant will meet the co-workers. He or she learns what the dress code involves, what schedule he or she will work, the collateral or related duties he or she must perform, and meets the other supervisors.

If the applicant-employee finds something objectionable, this is the time to speak up, because, in effect, the employer and employee are working out a verbal contract.

The employer is saying, "These are the tasks for which you are being hired. We have discussed your rate of pay, and this is what I expect you to do to earn that pay."

The employee may, at his or her option, either accept or reject the offer. However, if the employee accepts, he or she has no right to say at a later time that someone deluded him or her concerning the rate of pay, and what he or she must do to earn that pay.

And that's what indoctrination is. Once indoctrination is complete, training can begin.

Summary. There are those who say that the process we've described is too time-consuming—too complicated.

These same people will also say that turnover in their restaurants is at 200 or 300 percent.

A few years back, the last time figures were released, turnover in all American industry was at or near the six percent level.

In *well-run* restaurants, the figure was 66 percent. In poorly run restaurants, it was 300 percent. In other words, the *best* restaurants had personnel management policies that were only ten times worse than the average for American business.

Firing is caused by poor hiring. Employees must be dealt with on a professional level. They must be hired because they possess ability and talent, not because they were the first warm body to come through the door after the old employee quit in despair.

TRAINING
YOUR EMPLOYEES

Suggestion does not consist of
making one believe what is not true;
suggestion consists of
making something happen
by making one believe it is possible.

2

TRAINING YOUR EMPLOYEES

It is your business and system. Your manual of operations may be completely in your head, or it may be documented on reams of paper and visual aids. You do not have to use a lot of fancy trappings to train your employees.

You, the owner or manager, are the teacher. No one knows the business better than you. You fully realize you cannot operate the business by yourself. You need people to do your bidding. You, or someone equally capable, must explain and demonstrate what you want your personnel to do to give every guest the price-value relationship and eating experience that you have devised, so they will return again and again.

Maybe you're doing it now. Terrific! But even if you are, this section may shock you into becoming a better instructor by helping you realize how much more thorough the training you give your employees could be.

Here Come the Guests, Ready or Not

To expedite the noon rush, table setups were pulled from the closed-off back dining room. Next day, the store was hit with a big guest turnout. When they opened the back room, guess what? The tables were not set up.

☑ *B/L Recommends:* Teach hosts and hostesses to think ahead. Give them a checklist if necessary. Even little blunders cost money and customer rapport.

Private Eye

Name your favorite sleuth. From Sherlock Holmes, Charlie Chan and Ellery Queen to our modern day private detectives, *they all have the ability to see things* the untrained person will miss. Most managers are pretty good private eyes, too. Employees think good managers have eyes in the back of their heads. There's only one trouble—managers cannot be in all places at the same time. But *shouldn't someone be watching your customers?*

☑ *B/L Recommends:* Hire your own private eye to work your dining room and customer areas. Give this person only one duty. Train him or her to make personal and eye contact with every guest. This special *customer relations expert* should see to it that every guest is absolutely pleased with your service and quality. This special effects host or hostess can be your best business insurance for the minor expense of a few dollars per hour. Your specialist can protect your establishment and reputation.

Stopwatch Your People

Specialists have used time and motion studies to graph productivity and efficiency of employees. Their concern is to determine how many widgets can be produced (with fewest errors) in the shortest time. They consider time the most valuable commodity.

Foodservice people should also make advantageous use of time. Consider for a moment how much time our service personnel actually spend with guests. Fast fooders take and serve orders within seconds. Talk-time is limited to a few seconds. Cafeteria personnel may have no verbal contact with customers whatsoever. Coffee shop people turn tables in 25 to 35 minutes, and usually spend less than one minute in conversation with their customers. Dinnerhouse waiters and waitresses may serve guests for one or two hours, yet their actual total sales-talk time will be restricted to a minute or two.

☑ *B/L Recommends: Time is of the essence.* Teach your people what to do with their precious few moments with their guests. What they say can make or break a meal for the guest. Being alert, helpful, and concerned, and knowing when and when not to talk is an art.

Next time you conduct an employee meeting or chat with your help, discuss what they are saying, or not saying, to their guests. Demonstrate that each guest really receives only a moment's conversation—and what is said must count!

Customers Are Not Numbers

It's bad enough having Social Security numbers, credit cards and numbers for this and for that, and for everything we seem to do. Wherever we go, wherever we wait or stand in line for some product or service, what do we get? We get a damn number, that's what we get! Sociologists predict that all we may carry on our persons in the future in the way of money will be one personal serial number that can be used to record our purchases. Perhaps we will be ready for that when it happens. But what about for now? And should we carry this over into our foodservice businesses?

☑ *B/L Recommends:* Numbers are fine in a meat market, but we believe customers like to hear their own names whenever and as often as possible. Call it recognition. Call it courtesy. Numbers are cold and impersonal. Your foodservice establishment is, we hope, far from being impersonal. If anything, the only thing you may have to offer your guests that does not exist in your competitors' operations is *your personality,* and your ability to show your guests they are appreciated. There's no time like the present to change your habits into a system that will really produce extra sales and profits.

We proved our point when we convinced a fast food sandwich shop to switch from numbers to a first-name basis. The counter personnel literally beamed when we asked them to take orders and ask, "May I have your first name so I can call you when your order is ready?" The owner believes this added bit of friendliness definitely helped to increase sales and customer satisfaction. Make sure your personnel go out of their way to take and use your customers' names whenever possible.

Those Accursed To-go's

To-go orders take special handling in the galley. Cooks are not fond of to-go's. During rush periods, to-go's tend to break up the work rhythm in the fry station. Special handling degenerates to mishandling. To-go's seldom tip, so the serving force doesn't rejoice when asked to assemble to-go orders. This helps explain why a lot of to-go's leave the restaurant without proper accompaniments such as napkins, plastic forks, salt, pepper, and garnishes. When a to-go is called in, and the caller does not order from a to-go menu, a lot of time is wasted explaining what is on the menu. In fact, if to-go orders did not *provide such an attractive profit picture, and work to build business,* we'd say ignore this type of action.

☑ *B/L Recommends:* Convince your staff that *to-go orders are important to everybody's health and welfare.* A good to-go brings back customers. Back this up by providing the best available containers for preparing to-go's. Keep the containers in a clean, handy location. Hold school on what goes into which container. Conduct graduate instruction for people taking to-go orders. Customers often order items that are not suitable for to-go service. They think they have ordered a meal, but they pick up neo-garbage. Whoever handles to-go calls should be able to advise customers what is best in the to-go lineup. There should be a checklist at the to-go station to assure all required materials are placed in the to-go package. *Lastly, help the staff by preparing and distributing a simple to-go menu.* Feature items that keep well and only cause minor ripples in the food preparation work flow.

"I Wouldn't Order That if I Were You"

Haven't you been impressed (when dining out) by waiters and waitresses who suggested you *not* order a specialty of the house, or other dish? Didn't this added touch of personal sincerity encourage you to order something else; didn't you possibly leave an extra tip to show your appreciation for the "inside" information that helped you to make the best possible selection? Do your people suggest that your guest *not* order certain foods?

☑ *B/L Recommends:* We suggest you find out. This little game that service personnel can play can be used to extremes, and can cause some harm. It is a trick old pros use to garner extra tips and avoid handling certain dishes which they may find a nuisance. Guest check audits may not produce this type of specific information. We believe you should want to know if your personnel are practicing the *negative sell*. Their comments, while appearing to be cute, may also be injuring your total reputation. We have known waitresses to knock the efforts of certain cooks by telling guests the dish cannot be prepared properly. We have known waitresses to say, "I wouldn't order the special-of-the-day, if I were you," leaving the guest to wonder what was wrong with it. And, more often than you might think, cooks do become lazy. They will arbitrarily "86" certain items, thereby forcing service personnel to tell customers that those dishes are unavailable when, of course, they are available.

We have had experience with this problem. Years ago, when we owned and operated a 210-seat full service restaurant, we were told by our customers that our ice cream machines were always out of order. We knew this was not true. We were told that they could never seem to get what they ordered in the late evening. We checked and found that one of our waitresses had convinced the other waitresses to tell anyone who ordered any fancy ice cream specialties that our equipment was broken. They had become more concerned with their cleanup duties than with their guests. We nipped this attitude in the bud, and aside from reprimanding our crew, we posted a notice for everyone to read stating that our equipment was in perfect working order and would remain so, and that any further incidents of this sort would lead to an immediate dismissal. Our waitress apologized for being so thoughtless.

We also convinced everyone that to "86" anything was against our policy unless, of course, we were out of supply or an item was of poor quality. We further implemented a policy that stood the test of time, whereby it was mandatory for any person who had to "86" an item for any reason to document it on "86" lists, which were conveniently placed in the galley and service stations. In this manner we gave them every opportunity to be sincere with their guests while being straight with us. We convinced our crew to become more conscious of waste, improperly prepared items, poor quality, and unnecessary service gimmicks. *We proved that we meant to serve quality dishes*, and that we would do something constructive about any items that they would not order if they were the guest. Our caring made our people care. We wanted them to have respect for each other, the products and services each produced, and to work as a team.

Would You Like Anything Else? No?

No! Customers are *not* turned on when a service person asks such an open-minded question. This is not "suggestive selling." Lazy employees think they are asking for an additional order and sale. No way! They are wasting their time, your time, and the customer's time. Isn't there something that you are proud of? Are your foods so unattractive, tasteless, unappetizing, uninteresting, or overpriced as to be unworthy of mention by your people? Are you just too tired to keep after your salespeople to *sell*, and to really care that they offer their best efforts?

☑ *B/L Recommends:* You must train your people to present constructive, positive and effective sales points to each guest. They must believe in you, themselves, and the products which they have to offer.

Call your people together. Talk with them. Encourage a discussion concerning which foods they personally believe in and are proud to recommend. Find out what sort of suggestions they would appreciate hearing from their service person were they your guests and not your employees. Post a list of all positive and negative sales points, along with suggestions as to the best way to use them. Be sure everyone understands why guests should patronize your establishment. Believe us, you must be that basic. The majority of your people will be unaware of the quality, services, and price opportunities you offer. We have known too many employees (and managers) who were too lazy to recognize the extra fine qualities of their meats, batters, three-egg dishes, extra refills, homemade pies, soups, cakes, ice cream specialties, unique after dinner drinks, and other such "signature" items for which their operations are, or hope to become, famous.

You must convince your people to believe in the wonderful, exciting, interesting, delicious, attractive and wholesome food and beverage values that are available *only* in your house. Teach your people that "suggestive selling" is as simple as asking a guest if he or she would enjoy cream with the coffee. Then expand the thought to include other items that go well together to make a guest's eating experience more pleasurable. Customers like to say yes. You must see to it that your people say things that are intelligent, so your guests will have every opportunity to say *yes*.

They Won't Let Me Taste It

The scene: A party of six is seated and ready to order. They hesitate. Your waitress with pen and pad in hand waits to take the order. She offers a few helpful hints. A guest asks if one of the specialties of the house contains certain flavors. Your alert saleslady blurts back, "I don't know how it tastes—they won't let me eat it." Ouch! At almost every level and type of establishment, service personnel may speak the truth yet, unfortunately, with little common sense. Employees are products of their experiences.

☑ *B/L Recommends:* One of the most important things that you can do as a manager is to monitor what your people are saying to your customers. Prepare a list of questions with answers that have both negative and positive connotations. Discuss with your personnel the correct way to answer questions posed by their guests. With this specific example, periodically conduct a taste test to let your personnel eat what you want them to sell. Wine merchandisers have proved the value of wine-tasting clinics with groups of restaurant employees. Wine sales have zoomed, because service people know the correct answers, and know how to suggest wines with meals. You certainly can do the same with your foods.

Menu Education Is a Must for Service Personnel

Have you heard about the customer who asks the waitress, "What goes into the spaghetti al dente?" And the waitress replies, "I don't know, but I can ask the cook." That joke of a few years back has become a true-to-life description of what is going on in many stores today. Fewer and fewer foodservice personnel have accurate knowledge of the ingredients that make up menu items. It is a serious deficiency. In working in client stores, we see an increase in customer questions about the makeup of menu items. Also, we observe *fewer definitive answers being given by the foodservice staff.* Customers are asking these questions because there is a heightened awareness in this country of the importance of food and diet, and truth-in-menu restrictions have reduced the amount of informative material that used to appear on most menus. *Customers do not ask these questions for frivolous reasons.* The questions are important to them. A flip reply, or one that does not fully answer a customer's inquiry, is just as bad as any other aspect of poor customer service.

☑ *B/L Recommends: Develop a menu education program for serving personnel.* It is not enough to send a menu home with a waitress and expect that in a day or two she will be thoroughly knowledgeable on all the preparation techniques and food ingredients that make up menu offerings. Schedule short instruction periods during slow times in the galley, so that new waiters and waitresses can see and learn firsthand what goes into various dishes. Make sure serving personnel have a thorough grasp of the more exotic terms: "au jus," "sauté," "blanch," and so on. These terms are seldom heard in home kitchens. This type of knowledge has to be passed along in detail to the foodservice staff so that they know exactly what to say to guests. Employees should be instructed to avoid guessing when it comes to menu questions. Their professionalism is on the line.

Stressing a Sharp Appearance

A station that isn't properly lined up isn't going to do as much business as a station that is ready to go. *The same thing applies to personnel who work these stations*. A smartly turned out crew wins customer confidence. The confidence pays off in more repeat business and better tips for the crew. It can go the other way when managers neglect this area.

☑ *B/L Recommends:* Good grooming can be emphasized in many ways: by putting a full length mirror in the back of the store so personnel can check themselves before going on the floor; by a conscious effort on the part of the manager to compliment sharply turned out staff members; by maintaining a small stock of sundries, mouth washes, mints, hair spray, shoe polish for the use of personnel when necessary; by keeping a supply of uniform accessories on hand and on loan when needed. Helping personnel make a good appearance helps advertise your food and service at a very modest cost.

Stand up Straight

Remember how our parents used to nag and remind us not to slouch, and to stand erect? Good posture was considered as important as cleanliness. Boys all bent over were told they looked like old men. Girls who did not stand straight were considered ugly and poorly trained. One might even question their manners and other personality traits as being equally slouchy.

☑ *B/L Recommends: Correct posture is a must!* Teach your people to stand erect. Do not allow your service personnel to bend over and lean on tables and counter tops. Do not let them write their orders as though they were too tired to stand up. Customers do not appreciate people who lean over them. You certainly never purchased uniforms from a manufacturer's catalog in which the models were all hunched over. *Good posture sells merchandise.* Check your sales people.

Hooray and Boo

Do you subscribe to the interpersonal relationship philosophy that every compliment deserves a corresponding criticism? The person being complimented sooner than later catches on and waits for the axe to fall. The impact of the criticism can obscure the sincerity of the compliment. Yet employees should on appropriate occasions receive both forms of comment. *Employees want and need both forms of recognition.*

☑ *B/L Recommends:* Combine both do's and don'ts into an effective program for improvement. We encouraged one manager to try this technique with great success: He regularly reviews his guest checks to make sure his waiters and waitresses are writing, extending and totaling their items correctly. He prints a big "hooray" on many that are correct and a "boo" on those that are poorly written or inaccurate. His sense of humor is well accepted by the staff, who have taken the challenge to get more hoorays than boos. Naturally, the manager and his house are the winners. *Hooray for profits—Boo on losses.*

Food Waste Is a Way of Life with Youngsters

For 18 years or so, the kid has grown up around a home kitchen where a lot of food is thrown away. It is one of the facts of life in an abundant country. Then he goes to work in a restaurant and he sees more food wasted as guests leave scraps on their plates. He also notices huge quantities of food being delivered every day at the store's back door. So *how do you convince him that the waste or loss of food is harmful?* Or that the customer may discard food he or she paid for, but the restaurant cannot?

☑ *B/L Recommends:* Be blunt. Get the point across to young new employees that in restaurant operations, food is money. *Stealing or giving away food is the same as stealing money from the store.* For some reason, a lot of juveniles accept what they call a "rip-off" as merely a naughty expression of individuality. Do not use the term in talking to young employees, use the hard words "thievery, pilferage, stealing." Make sure the new person is thoroughly aware of the painful consequences if he or she mishandles the restaurant's food or cash.

We and Katherine Hepburn Have Something in Common

When interviewed on the Dick Cavett Show, this great actress said *people should be very concerned about how they sound.* We could not agree more. After all, we and our people are on stage when in front of customers.

☑ *B/L Recommends:* Show your crew that you own a tape recorder. Use it to record, among other things, the noises, voices, and even arguments that can be heard in your store.

We situated our tape recorder on the pass-bar between the dining room and the kitchen area of one establishment to prove to the owner that there was chaos at this critical point in his operation. He was so used to the call-in method of ordering that he was unaware of the confusion and din that several voices can generate. Employees on both sides of the counter at the order area repeated, argued about, and clarified their orders. Drag orders (orders that have not come up together) were abundant. We played the tape back to him and members of his crew. He was convinced. He needed a guest check system that would eliminate the upsetting confusion and actual loss of food orders.

You can use a tape recorder to train your personnel and record their sales presentations. Remember, your people are on stage, and as good actors and actresses they should rehearse their lines to sell your script (menu) to more paying customers and standing-room-only crowds.

In Defense of the Four-Letter Word

The four-letter words we choose to defend are those like "work" or "duty" or "love" or "good." There are some others we could choose not to defend. Some deal with bodily functions, bodily waste, or interpersonal relationships, and hardly seem appropriate to the restaurant atmosphere. It was well said many years ago: *"The use of profanity indicates an inadequate vocabulary."*

☑ *B/L Recommends:* Communication is vital to the success of the restaurant, but a *"f------ spatula"* is no more efficient than a *plain spatula*. *"That s---"* is no more descriptive than *that material*. There are hardly any businesses in the world that deal with their customers on a more personal level. They expect sanitation and wholesomeness in their food and surroundings. It would seem reasonable to provide the same qualities in the language of those who operate the restaurants.

Life in the Dog House

The assistant manager was a dog lover—a serious, dedicated, committed dog lover. In all innocence, he told the service assistants to save meat scraps and bones from their plates. After all, his dogs deserved the best. The customers heard the assistant give the instructions, and later, customers heard the service assistants commenting on the new instructions. *They assumed that the meat scraps would be served in tomorrow's specials*. The owner had a tough time putting down that rumor.

☑ *B/L Recommends:* Murphy's Law states: "Anything that can go wrong, will." O'Brien's Addendum says: "Murphy was an optimist." It seems that the millions of dollars that are spent advertising the positive things about a business turn out to be totally ineffective in the face of one piece of bad news. *It must be continually remembered and emphasized that we are totally visible on the floor,* and everything we do or say is subject to interpretation by our customers. We are actors on a stage, and if we ad-lib, we're going to have to pay the price when the show folds.

Catch 'Em with the Ketchup

Once every so often do you look at your operation from the customer's point of view? Have you developed a case of tunnel vision? Are you so numb and used to routine that you have neglected to recognize certain bad habits of your personnel?

☑ *B/L Recommends:* Watch your service personnel do a balancing act with the ketchup bottles—*right in front of your customers!* Emptying several bottles into another bottle in full view takes away from the image we are sure you want to convey. We are not suggesting you stop this practice. Just do not allow it to be done out in the open, on the pass bar, counter, or in the service station. Do it in the rear areas of your store! By the way, it can be a dangerous practice. Glass chips can break off and fall into the ketchup bottle that is being refilled. Be careful.

The 20 Questions Routine

There are questions that must be asked so the guest's order can be prepared correctly. There are other questions that just generate irritation. Guests who enjoy steak sauce are a little annoyed when the waiter or waitress asks, "Would you like steak sauce?" *Of course they would, they have liked it all their lives.* Guests feel they are paying for a meal with the appropriate extras, not for an interrogation.

☑ *B/L Recommends:* Discourage condiment quiz games. *Make the serving of standard condiments automatic.* We have seen waiters and waitresses quiz customers during rush periods, then promptly forget what it was the customer wanted. Holding back condiments saves pennies at the risk of revenue dollars.

An Issue That Should Not Be Tabled

Sautéed concrete is a slow mover as a menu item. Then again, *if tabletops are not cleared and cleaned efficiently during rush periods*, warm concrete will produce as much profit as anything on the menu. It is strange how an investment of thousands of dollars in kitchen equipment and crew training can be thrown for a loss by a few dirty dishes and a little trash. It is a situation that affects all operations from fast fooders to full service units.

☑ *B/L Recommends:* Management must concentrate on clearing tabletops as fast and thoroughly as possible in peak periods. *Nobody on the floor should be exempt from performing this function.* All front end trainees should be made aware that clearing tables is a matter of top priority.

Heroes in a Snowstorm

Give your employees the opportunity and they will *go under* rather than call for assistance. You have no doubt heard your people at times complain that they are "snowed"—meaning they have more work than they can properly handle. Yet, what do they do? They continue to try to work out of their predicament without calling for help from you or their fellow workers. Being a hero is poor judgment in our book. Your customers should not be the ones to suffer with poor quality foods and service because your employees cannot handle their stations. True, they will often work harder and faster whenever they get into trouble, but usually work more sloppily when they panic. Is there a reason why they will go it alone rather than ask for assistance? Have you, their manager, made them feel guilty every time they find themselves in a predicament?

☑ *B/L Recommends:* It is a manager's responsibility to create teamwork and cooperation. We have seen cooks, for example, go under with some 20 checks on their order wheel when the whole dining room numbered only 30 tables. When two-thirds of your house are seated but not eating you have a problem. Beware of a chain reaction. Your cooks may be the first to be snowed, but in a matter of moments (depending upon the speed of your kitchen) your service personnel will be the next ones to go under. Their orders will come up together, too fast. Imagine a waitress with five tables on her station, with 15 to

20 customers waiting to be served, having to pick up and deliver all her dishes virtually at once to avoid cold food and customer dissatisfaction. She will be the one to receive the dirty looks and complaints.

Why take a chance? Your best defense is to watch your people and *step in before they let themselves get swamped*. Place colored tape on your pass shelf and order wheels as a warning line for your cooks. Whenever their guest check orders reach that point they are not to guess or think. Their instructions should be to call for immediate assistance—and avoid a "snowstorm."

How Hot Should Soup Be?

A lot of soup is sold from soup wells, *but not much of it is hot*. Soup should be hot enough to scald the unwary. Nobody ever complained about burning their tongue on hot food, but they sure complain about cold food.

☑ *B/L Recommends:* Put hot water into the hot food warmer and turn the power up to medium or better. (All food warmer controls react differently.) Put an inset of hot soup into the hot food warmer. (Don't depend on the warmer to heat it.) Cover the soup, and *cuss at anybody who leaves the cover off*. (A cover prevents evaporation and holds the heat better.) Use warm soup bowls if possible. (A cold bowl chills the soup.) Rush to the table while the soup is hot.

When They Guess—You Can't Win

Every item you serve has its own measure in weight, size, portion control, and cost. If your crew has to play a guessing game as to how you want things done, *you will lose money*. An active portion control program is vital to any foodservice operation. It need not cost a lot of money; it doesn't require a bunch of threats either. Your crew will do what is right if you place proper and continuing emphasis on the how's and why's of portion control. This should be delegated to everyone up and down the line. A portion control program specifies which ladle, scoop, glass, and plate is to be used in the preparation and service of every item on your menu.

☑ *B/L Recommends:* Sketch or photograph each food item. Prepare simple explanations of what goes where, and how, and paste them beneath the photos. Post the material on your bulletin board or in the kitchen area. When things go wrong and portion controls are not being followed, don't be the usual kind of boss who complains that you *told* them how to do it. Do not just tell them—show them with aids they can refer to when you are not standing next to them. Make the subject of portion control a part of every meeting you conduct with your people on an individual or group basis.

Create a preparation chart listing every item that requires preparation on your menu. Extend the lines across the chart and place the names of each employee who has the responsibility to prepare your food on a separate line. Give all who can prepare your items properly and beautifully as much personal recognition as possible. Gold stars on the bulletin board charts or even small cash awards given out at employee sales meetings will show you appreciate this professionalism. Employees will work hard to earn their awards and gold stars when they see their buddies earn them.

Origin of the "Tip"

It seems the time-honored tradition of tipping began in Rome and became formalized in eighteenth century England when innkeepers started hanging boxes under signs labeled "T.I.P." meaning; "To Insure Promptness—Eat Here."

☑ *B/L Recommends:* "T.I.P." has in many instances lost its meaning to many service personnel. Management could use the initials "To ImPress" on everyone what tipping really means, why tips are given, and how to earn them.

The Sale That Got Away

Your guests have just spent from 60 cents to over 60 dollars with you. Their eating experience was a pleasant one, in keeping with your quality/service/price concept. The situation is the same whether yours is a fast fooder that feeds customers in seconds, a cafeteria where guests serve themselves up to a point, a caterer who is responsible for a complete dinner, or an establishment where the entree alone may take over 30 minutes to prepare—your guests are willing to pay for whatever it is you consider to be a complete value. But *that's the question: What is a complete value?*

☑ *B/L Recommends: Be certain your personnel complete the required service for every guest.* Counter people must be sure that orders are complete to the smallest detail. They only have seconds in which to do it. Other houses can take up to an hour or more to sell, service, pull tables, and present the tab.

Whatever your strategy is to move guests in and out, all guests should receive complete service *until they depart.* Improperly trained and unmotivated employees believe that once the check has been presented or paid, they have finished their job and responsibilities to their guests. Not true! Allowing guests to sit with dirty dishes and empty water glasses in front of them is an indication of incomplete service.

Everyone who works behind your counter or in your dining room has a responsibility to convince your guests to return often. Guests will, if their last impression is a good one. If your service stops when the guest is presented with a check, or pays, you are losing sales.

Everything Is Not All Right with This Question

When it comes to dumb questions, our favorite is one the cashier asks: *"Was everything all right?"* Generally she or he appears as interested in the answer as in the weather forecast for Outer Mongolia. That's why she or he asks the question while looking directly into the cash drawer. The public relations genius who thought up this gambit left the job half done. The other half can get tricky: *"No. Everything was not all right!"* What happens when the customer gives this response? We tried this out on two cashiers last week. The first commiserated with us: "Gee, that's too bad." The other said, with little optimism, "We'll try to do better next time." *What next time, lady?* For adding insult to injured customer relations, this type of reply is almost as effective as keeping a tire slasher in the parking lot.

☑ *B/L Recommends:* Don't permit cashiers to ask leading questions. When they do, the customer and the cashier both have to make judgments. *Somebody is going to suffer additional aggravation.* Have cashiers make friendly, positive statements; tell 'em cashstand quiz shows don't pay off.

School for Hypocrites?

Nobody came out and said it, during the hiring, but the new managers were given the message that there would be no cash shortages in the register—overages were all right, but shortages were not. Shortages would have to be made up, one way or another. Inexperienced or naive managers made up the shortages from their pockets. Those with more experience collected from the cashiers and waitresses. The really sharp ones created a "slush fund" from overages, to take care of shortages. In attempting to do what was perceived as management's wish, *the entire cash handling and accounting system became a cynical, dishonest game,* in which everybody lost both cash and honor.

☑ *B/L Recommends:* The first thing to do is admit that people make mistakes—some on the plus side, and some on the minus. *Every mistake is an announcement that additional training is required.* Cover-ups are like a band-aid at a beheading. Cover-ups help thieves beat the system, by hiding theft in the middle of deceit. Overages and shortages point out that additional cash controls may be necessary. Cover-ups hide the problem until the entire structure crumbles around you.

Where Does All the Money Go?

It's pretty much a fact of life that few employees know what happens to all the cash in the register. For that matter, a significant number of managers do not fully understand the relationship between income and expenses.

Few employees have ever had in their possession the thousands of dollars that go into a restaurant's cash register. They think that the owner must be as rich as an oil sheikh. About the only thing they know about cost is the statements that are always made about food cost. They would never think of payroll as an expense—that's their income. Rent, taxes, utilities, insurance, supplies are all too remote to be considered.

An employee's lack of understanding of basic economics can lead to jealousy. Jealousy can lead to a desire for revenge. This takes the form of theft, waste, vandalism, and very poor public relations.

Constructive management and modern leadership techniques can reverse this feeling. In one dramatic meeting, management can graphically demonstrate some of the hard realities of restaurant operations in these inflationary times. The purpose of the meeting is to break down the profit and loss statement (P&L) into clearly understood terms.

It would serve little purpose to post the P&L on the bulletin board, or read it to crew members at a meeting. Something else must be done to burn the facts into the memory of each person on the payroll.

☑ *B/L Recommends:* Set the stage for one of the most important subjects that you can cover. You'll need:

1) A blackboard, chalk, and eraser
2) A large mixing bowl
3) A copy, or dummied copy, of the P&L
4) One hundred silver dollars

And, of course the usual supply of chairs, ashtrays, coffee, and whatever is normal in your meetings. This is how the meeting is to be conducted:

A) Take care of all the routine business quickly, while interest is still high.
B) Invite a member of the crew to assist. Give your assistant a bag containing one hundred silver dollars to hold.
C) Tell the employees that the silver dollars represent a hundred dollars from the register.
D) Tell the employees that the money in the register includes sales taxes, so have your assistant count out four, five, or six dollars and drop them into the mixing bowl.
E) Tell the employees that food and beverage costs come out of the cash in the register. Have your assistant count out 32 or 35, or 40 dollars, or whatever your food cost percentages may be. Drop these into the bowl.
F) Explain about payroll expenses and payroll taxes. Have your assistant drop silver dollars for the labor cost, and more silver dollars for the taxes paid on payroll.
G) Go on through the P&L, demonstrating the costs for rent, taxes, supplies, insurance, laundry, maintenance, and so on. When all the expenses are paid according to the figures on the P&L, what's left is profit. Have your assistant hand you the silver dollars that represent profit.
H) Tell the employees that the money you hold is all the profit the restaurant provides out of every hundred dollars taken in, but even that isn't the end of the story.
I) Show how much goes to pay income taxes and social security. Show how much goes to repay the loan that permitted the establishment of the business.

J) Hold up the few dollars that represent clear profit.

At this point, the operation of economics in this restaurant has been demonstrated in a way that leaves nothing to the imagination.

As a final way of impressing the lesson on the crew members, tell them that every bit of waste or breakage means that the restaurant suffers. Suppose, for instance that the amount of profit remaining was three dollars. Drop a three dollar plate on the floor and tell the employees that the next one hundred dollars in sales will just barely cover the cost of the plate. Until the plate has been paid for, the owner is working for nothing, even though the employees remain on full pay.

Any subject such as this must be demonstrated graphically, or it serves no purpose except to put the employees to sleep. When they see the silver dollars filling the bowl (the expenses), when they see how few remain in the form of profit, and when the manager deliberately breaks that plate, they have been given more than enough reason to act with good judgment in the handling of food, equipment, and supplies.

What Is 1% of $3,500?

Simple. The answer is $350, or is it $.35? No, it is $35.00. One percent, or a multiple of it can add up to quite a bit of money when it represents an excessive cost of food or labor. The first thing a manager must know is how to figure percentages and interpret them as dollars.

One young man we recently interviewed with a client failed to correctly answer the above question. He wanted a management position. He said he previously had been in charge of a fast food unit, and had been responsible for the profits, food and labor costs, etc. He said he had recently graduated from a local trade school of restaurant management. Apparently they had not taught (or he did not learn) how to compute simple figures. How about you? Are you reasonably good with numbers, percentages, and dollars?

☑ *B/L Recommends:* Professionals are not fools. They know how to figure the numbers that are important to their businesses. You can only bluff your way for so long. Dig out an old math book, buy one, or check one out at your local library. Learn how to accurately arrive at your correct numbers. Next, *do not just talk percentages* to your superiors or subordinates. It is a trap to do so. *Talk money!* One percent of something does not sound like much, but a few points can really add up to very important dollars. Another chain store manager offered us a list of excuses why he had over-bought and over-staffed his unit. He considered a total of some ten percentage points as his investment in training and inventory. We might normally accept such an argument were it not for the fact that his figures were consistently running too high. We helped him to break down his percentages into dollars. His problem: He did not relate the two. His overages were in excess of five hundred dollars per week. That is a lot of groceries and payroll for one unit. This manager had to shape up quickly or receive what we call his "D.C.M."—Don't Come Monday.

A National Cashier Test—for All Reasons

Research has shown that average untrained foodservice employees who handle cash, process guest checks and customer orders, commit in excess of a 20 percent error factor in simple arithmetic extension. When employees make a mistake, it is your money they lose! It takes discipline, training, and a firm desire on your part to substantially reduce the frequency of errors and resultant losses caused by your personnel.

☑ *B/L Recommends:* Issue our National Cashier Test to each of your employees. Block out the answers printed at the bottom of page 31. Keep for your confidential use. It makes little difference what you feature on your menu or the prices you charge. See how well your people can do with these ten questions. Make a big thing about those who score a perfect 100 percent. Compliment them. You might even care to offer a small token cash award for perfection to show your appreciation. Make it a game. Yet be serious. Importantly, issue a test to all new employees from now on before you allow them to get their hands on your cash and guest checks. You may find, as did we, that some people just cannot handle simple math and foodservice price combinations. Doesn't it make a great deal of *cents* to find out now if your people can add and subtract?

NATIONAL CASHIER TEST

Name _____ Date _____

Unit _____ **SCORE** _____

TO: ALL PERSONNEL WHO HANDLE CASH, GUEST CHECKS, CHARGES, AND CUSTOMER ORDERS:

Dear Ladies and Gentlemen: By taking your position, you have accepted the responsibility to do one or more of the following: accept cash, operate a cash register, make change, take orders, complete guest checks, and extend and total orders without error. To undercharge will certainly hurt your store, company, and ultimately your own pay check. To overcharge will hurt your most important asset—your customers. The following questions represent typical problems which foodservice personnel see every day. Thousands of people will be taking this test. How many questions can you answer correctly? There are no tricks. *Do not compute or charge taxes.* There are ten questions, each with a value of ten points. A perfect score is 100 (100 percent).

1.   These columns represent four guest checks that service personnel forgot to add. The guests are waiting to pay. You are the cashier. Please show the correct totals:

$0.89	$1.75	$6.95	$ 7.25
0.55	2.95	3.75	8.95
0.27	1.25	4.85	10.75
1.19	0.60	0.90	11.50
0.65	3.55	5.35	1.20
$	$	$	$

2.   Your customer questions the total. You must quickly extend each item to determine if a mistake exists. Show each extension and the correct total:

Two Hamburger Sandwiches @ $1.65 each .... $ _____
Two Malted Milk Shakes @ $0.85 each .... $ _____
Two Orders of Onion Rings @ $0.90 each .... $ _____
Two Pieces of Pie @ $0.55 each .... $ _____

                        Total .... $ _____

3.   Three businessmen requested separate checks but did not receive them. They ask you, the cashier, to charge them separately. You smile and say you will be happy to do so. The check shows a total of *$18.95.* It is correct. Show what each guest must pay:

Man # 1: Special Plate, $4.95, Coffee $0.50,
   Dessert $1.25 .... $ _____
Man #2: Steak Sandwich $5.85, Salad $0.75,
   Glass of Wine $0.85 .... $ _____
Man #3: Diet Plate $3.65, Half Grapefruit $0.65,
   Coffee $0.50 .... $ _____

4.   Nine young men want to split the check evenly. Their guest check total is *$17.01.* Specify how much each must pay: $ _____

5.   The bill at the Country Club for 4 dinners came to *$46.70.* The rules of the Club specify that management will add on a service charge of 15%. Supply two answers:

(a) How much money is the service charge? .... $ _____
(b) What is the complete new total? .... $ _____

6.   A regular customer telephones in a to-go order. She asks you the total so she can send her son to pick up the order and pay with a check made out in the correct amount. You cheerfully accept, extend, and total the order:

6 Chili Dogs @ $0.89 each .... $ _____
3 Plain Dogs @ $0.59 each .... $ _____
4 Large Cokes @ $0.49 each .... $ _____
3 Small Orange Drinks @ $0.29 each .... $ _____
2 Root Beer Floats @ $0.79 each .... $ _____

                              Total .... $ _____

7.   You are taking cash. A guest presents a guest check in the amount of *$20.35,* and a *$20.00* bill for payment. The customer complains the waiter did not deliver the salad priced at *$1.25.* You accept the complaint. You deduct the full price of the salad and give the guest his change. How much change do you return? $_____

8.   You are a waitress in a pizza house. A large group orders just about everything in sight. Your guest check is covered with so many words and figures that you decide to rewrite it. Show the correct extensions and the total the group should pay:

2 Large Pizzas (No Anchovies) @ $5.75 each .... $ _____
2 Combination Pizzas (Medium—with 6 items)
    @ $6.85 each .... $ _____
3 Spaghetti Dinners @ $3.45 each .... $ _____
3 Special Dinners @ $5.85 each .... $ _____
3 Mixed Green Salads (For two persons) @ $1.90 each $ _____
5 Coffees @ $0.40 each .... $ _____
3 Soft Drinks @ $0.49 each .... $ _____
2 Iced Teas @ $0.49 each .... $ _____
4 Ice Creams @ $0.85 each .... $ _____

                              Total .... $ _____

9.   A party of six consumes 6 Special Dinners—each regularly priced at *$4.95.* The dinners are complete except for the beverages which the guests order separately. Their beverage order comes to *$1.50.* They present 3 coupons "As Advertised" offering "2 Special Dinners for the Price of 1" to you along with their payment. How much should you charge them for the dinners *and* the beverages as ordered? Total: $ _____

10. Two customers order the following: 2 Buckets of Chicken @ $7.69 each, 2 Pints of Cole Slaw @ $ .79 each, 6 orders of French Fries @ $0.39 per order, and 8 Large Soft Drinks @ $0.47 each. The customers present two coupons good for "$1.00 Off on a Bucket of Chicken." The coupons are in order. How much should the customers pay for the full order of food and beverages after you allow the discount? Total: $_____

Note: Please ask your manager to check your answers. Professionals should score a perfect 100 percent. Had you been using real money and your score was less than perfect, you would have lost important sales and profits for your establishment. Shortages can break a foodservice operation if everyone is not as careful as possible. THANK YOU FOR TAKING THIS CASHIER TEST.

CONFIDENTIAL . . . Block out these answers before giving test to personnel!

(1) 3.55, 10.10, 21.80, 39.65
(2) 3.30, 1.70, 1.80, 1.10 = 7.90
(3) 6.70, 7.45, 4.80
(4) 1.89 each
(5) 7.00 = 53.70

(6) 5.34, 1.77, 1.96, .87, 1.58 = 11.52
(7) .90
(8) 11.50, 13.70, 10.35, 17.55, 5.70, 2.00, 1.47, .98, 3.40 = 66.65
(9) 16.35
(10) 21.06

YOUR RELATIONS
WITH YOUR PERSONNEL

The open mouth
and the closed mind
make a treacherous pair.

3

YOUR RELATIONS WITH YOUR PERSONNEL

Only hermits can get along on their own; those of us in food service need people as customers and employees. We all need the recognition due us as unique human beings who have much we can contribute to our jobs to help our fellow workers and guests. Many of us are quite willing to respond positively when we are approached in the right way.

Personnel relations are our most challenging responsibility. Our total success is the result of how well we deal with superiors, peers, and subordinates. Profits and a return on our investment may be our goals, but the name of the game is people.

We often tell our personnel that they, like actors, are on stage and highly visible to their guests; therefore they must always be on their best behavior. Similarly, we in management are perceived by both our guests and personnel as being either terrific leaders or lousy bosses.

A sharp, well-informed, smoothly performing team is a direct reflection of its leadership. Personnel pointers in the following section can help you become the finest leader, a leader people will want to work for just because you are thoughtful enough to say such simple things as "thank you," and "please."

When "Tough Harley" Talks, Managers Walk

For a long time, "Tough Harley," the area supervisor, reveled in his renown as a rugged executive-type. He made it clear he did not believe in coddling unit managers or crews. One of his favorite tactics was to call shift managers in for a meeting on their day off. *He never gave a reason*, just a warning: "that manager damned well better not be late!" Since it was well-known that nothing good ever came out of a meeting with the area supervisor, managers would occasionally quit rather than put up with the aggravation. Others dropped out after a session or two with "Tough Harley." This convinced old T.H. he was doing the right thing—weeding out malcontents and weaklings. His only mistake was to brag to a company vice president that he was so good at making his people perform when he snapped his fingers. The company ran a records check on personnel turnover. They learned "Tough Harley" was in effect, *operating a tremendous training school for all the competing chains in his area*. It was actually costing the company thousands of dollars to supply well-trained junior leadership to the competition. What Harley's company had left was a collection of thoroughly cowed white-knucklers living in dread of any communication with company management.

☑ *B/L Recommends:* Obtuse managers and executives have to be made aware that personnel are a company asset the same as the company bank account and all the equipment it owns. *All three are vital to the welfare and growth of the firm*. Mistreat any one of these elements and the others suffer almost as badly.

Teach 'Em, Don't Threaten 'Em

The unit manager was trying to get some guidance on implementing a new employee directive. The district manager became exasperated when he couldn't answer the questions. "If you don't like it, you know where the door is," he told the unit man. To make the point stick, he added, "don't let the door hit you in the butt on the way out." *This type of middle management arrogance is extremely expensive*. The result is that new unit managers have to be constantly hired and trained. Policies are seldom carried through the way the top echelon intended.

☑ *B/L Recommends:* Competent translation of policies is the job of middle management. Nothing positive is accomplished when district or regional managers exert authority instead of good sense.

Management by Fear

The owner of the restaurant refused to believe that crew members were terrified of him. He called in a waitress and demanded to know whether she were afraid of him. Of course, she said "no," and *he shouted at us that we didn't know what we were talking about*. We used a 35mm camera and very fast film to take candid shots of the owner in action. When he saw the frowning, snarling, arm-waving, and domineering way he worked, he admitted that we *might* be right.

☑ *B/L Recommends:* Sometimes forcefulness is misinterpreted as bullying; sometimes concentration is confused with rejection; sometimes professionalism is mistaken for arrogance. *Sometimes we fail to note how our behavior is read,* or misread, by those who depend on us.

Courtesy Has a Cash Value

"Get me iced coffee," the manager told the waitress. Then, ignoring both the coffee and the waitress, the manager commenced reciting a list to us of the difficulties the store was experiencing. He did not have to spell things out; he had already presented one graphic example. *The manager did not know how to say "please" and "thank you."* While the employees were told to be courteous to guests—on pain of dismissal—the manager assumed the standard did not apply to himself when dealing with employees. As the store's problems mounted, the employees' desire to help out diminished.

☑ *B/L Recommends:* Keep in mind: Employees go home at night. *Whether they come to work the next day or not, depends largely on incentive.* "Good morning," "please," and "thank you" are small tokens of management's appreciation of a worker's contribution to the business. These tokens do not cost a whole lot, so spend them freely.

Sarcasm—the Bad Mouth Habit

"The tongue can ruin reputation, defeat ambition, disgrace others, and double-cross its owner." We believe it.

Managers, to be effective, must have the respect of their help. We generally cannot attract it if we bad-mouth our people, our management, or our customers. How often have we seen a waitress arrive on shift to be greeted by a wisecracking manager who thinks he's a real joker. You recognize this scenario: the waitress showers, carefully applies her makeup, dresses, does her best to look attractive and presentable, arrives for work and is greeted with a "hello ugly" comment from her manager. This may break him up. He sure loses points with this employee and others who may have been within earshot. Other snide remarks like baldy, fatso, or boy, and ethnic slurs rarely win friends and influence people.

☑ *B/L Recommends:* We must respect ourselves and our people. No longer should male managers refer to women as "broads," or to personnel as "bodies." Be careful. Do not use sarcasm to attract attention. Our society is negative enough without our helping to put everyone down. You must know how it feels. Why hurt others, especially when you want them to really make an effort for you?

Introducing: A Tactic That Improves Teamwork

It costs money to use certain terms on the job. One of the most expensive is, "I'll have somebody show you around." The price tag on this sentence is seldom less than $50.00; frequently it is a lot more. The statement is made by managers who consider it beneath their dignity to take a newly hired person around to meet the rest of the crew. At the minimum, this means the new employee is going to have a longer, tougher time adjusting to the job. The store has to pay for this unproductive period and for all the miscues that go with it. Based upon what transpires during the introductory phase, the new employee may elect not to become a part of the organization at all. *It is a very sensitive time in this person's life*. At the same time, most operations have a couple of tough characters on the staff capable of saying things that would make a drill sergeant blush.

☑ *B/L Recommends:* When the pool has sharks in it, don't use a sink-or-swim approach with new employees. *Properly introduced, employees become part of the team much faster*. This translates into better revenues for the store, smaller work load for the staff. Make sure this latter point is clearly understood by the old-timers. The new employee needs help, not hazing.

Let's Retire the Busboys

Busboys represent the restaurant industry's greatest anachronism. They should be eliminated as a class. These days, males and females are doing the job. As we all know, the word "boy" is pejorative, unless you mean somebody in the Cub Scouts.

Not only does the title need to be scrapped, so does the thinking that goes along with it. Ever since the position came into being it has been classed as unskilled labor. *It is anything but that*. It takes skill to maximize a restaurant's profitability during rush periods. A restaurant does not make the money it should unless there is an orderly, efficient movement of food, equipment and supplies into and out of the dining area. A restaurant does not make the money it should if the process has to be closely and constantly supervised by someone in a higher pay bracket than the person doing the job. Consequently, in today's restaurant scheme of things, where profitability depends on close tolerances between food, labor, and volume, *few restaurants can afford to operate with old-style busboys*. The job has to be filled by people who know what they are doing and why. They have to be capable of evaluating conflicting priorities and taking appropriate action without specific instruction.

☑ *B/L Recommends: Consider hiring and training "Service Assistants."* This title may be applied to employees of either sex filling the job. The title upgrades the position and more accurately reflects the functions performed in the modern restaurant. The next thing to do is write down what you expect your service assistants to do—a job description. It seems simple: you want them to clean tables, get the soiled tableware to the dishwasher, clean the booth area and get it set up for the next party. And you want it done quickly.

Here's where it starts to get complicated. You have only a certain inventory of tableware on the floor. On cold days soup bowls and spoons come in for heavy usage; the service assistant has to be aware of this so orders don't get stalled in the kitchen. Or, the restaurant runs a steak platter special. What happens if the service assistant doesn't give platters priority attention? *It kills the floor.* There are a lot of dollars at stake just in training service assistants in the proper way to handle this one basic duty. Then there are other tasks: The S.A. may be expected to deliver water to the table, care for articles of clothing handed over by guests, aid the waiter or waitress in the delivery of the order by carrying excess plates, trays and tray racks. There are table condiments to be put in place, coffee refills, breads, butters, sauces and garnishes to be presented. *All this is related to guest satisfaction.*

There is money at stake. The work is too important to be left to unskilled, untrained people. We've only looked at about one tenth of the specified duties of an S.A. at this point. What we are saying is that a well-trained service assistant is a big asset to any operation. If you impress the S.A.'s with their responsibilities, and acknowledge they have some prestige in the restaurant hierarchy, Service Assistants will do a better job and stay with you longer than old-fashioned busboys.

Employees Have Needs Too!

Are you more interested in production or *people?* You know how to produce your foods. You are more at home in this area than you are "out front" in your establishment. You concentrate on every detail: purchase, measure, preparation, yield, serving. Perhaps you believe you can guarantee your profits from the back of your house. Neglect your people, and you may be well on your way to achieving poor employee morale and, ultimately, decreased productivity.

☑ *B/L Recommends:* Make a deal with yourself right now: Agree to exert an equal amount of effort in getting to know your people as in your technical work. You had better believe that tests and studies have shown the following: A) Employees need to feel important. B) They need to feel they are members of a team. C) Employees need to understand the significance of their contribution to their jobs and to their stores. D) They need to feel they are receiving fair pay and fair treatment. E) Employees need to have superiors who will listen to their gripes. F) Last, but not least, they need to feel they have suggestions that may be worthwhile for the good of *your* organization and their store.

Please note: These suggestions—these *employee needs*—apply to "mom and pop" stores and small independents just as much as they do to larger operations.

Happy Birthday to _____

Have you ever had a birthday come and go without so much as one birthday wish from a friend or relative? Sad, isn't it? To be a member of a family and to be forgotten and neglected on your own special day is no fun. Mommy and Daddy never forgot!

☑ *B/L Recommends:* Managers, owners and co-workers often become something like family to one another. You should not forget or neglect any of your people on their special days. You have their applications. Their birth-dates are listed on them. Surprise employees with a cake, a bunch of flowers, a day off (with or without pay), a mention on the bulletin board and blackboard for employees and customers to see. Do something nice. It need not cost you much at all. *It's the thought that counts.* Turn this saying around and you may find that thoughtless people do *not* count. Good bosses—good leaders—may be tough and demanding, but they are *never* thoughtless.

Don't Say "No" to Productivity

A chief executive of a highly successful restaurant company has a unique claim to fame. He says he has never turned down a constructive suggestion from one of his employees. The trick, he claims, is in taking an idea apart and going over it piece by piece. *Somewhere in the parts there is bound to be something worthwhile.* Seemingly useless suggestions, aimed at symptoms instead of causes, can trigger improvements. One example he cites is the case of a back-up man who asked for a new type of slicer to help him keep up with all his work. The slicer was expensive and there was really no practical place to install it. In going over the request, it was found that over several months the cooks had been quietly unloading chores on the back-up man. If the slicer request had been given an immediate rejection, as was logical, the restaurant would have lost a valuable employee. The back-up man felt he couldn't handle the job any longer. Without the slicer, he felt the only thing he could do was quit. Instead, there was a realignment of duties and a significant improvement in production.

☑ *B/L Recommends:* Listen carefully to what employees are trying to tell you. Managers with a one-way approach to getting things done are like people trying to buy something with Monopoly money. All they are going to realize is a lot of lost time. *Employees respond with productivity when they know management appreciates their work and their ideas.*

Brainstorming Your Way to Better Profits

The difficulty with being in a rut is that you are below *see* level. You can't see many opportunities for improving business and profits. Friends and relatives usually toss ideas around like confetti. Most of their ideas carry about the same weight as those tiny specks of colored paper. Well-intentioned as these folks are, they do not really know and understand your business. If you suspect you are slipping into a business rut, consider turning to the experts, the people that know the business and know a little about you. *These experts can produce some practical ideas and can make them work.* It's not expensive to get expert guidance—you know how much you pay your employees. They are experts at what they do or they wouldn't be your employees. All it takes to elicit their expertise is some sincere effort.

☑ *B/L Recommends:* Bring together your management team or employee group. Set the proper scene and mood. Get rid of the basic business matters as quickly as possible. Pass around slips of paper and pencils. Ask each person to write down his or her suggestions on any subject relevant to operations, employees, guests, expenses, profits, or advertising.

Carefully define your objectives to the group: You are seeking new ideas, and ways to improve procedures. After everybody has his or her suggestions written out, read the ideas to the group and ask them to vote on the relative merits of each proposal. Tell the group that they will not be permitted to counter the suggestions with defensive arguments; the point of the exercise is to consider all suggestions with open mind.

As you read the suggestions to the group, omit any references to individual names that may appear in the text. Present the idea only; do not say who authored the thought. This will avoid any bias in respect to time on the job, age, sex, etc. As you read the material, discard the items that do not seem to excite or impress the group. Keep sharp discipline. Move the meeting along briskly to get everyone's ideas before the panel. Keep the meeting spirited and positive.

End your brainstorming session by thanking all the participants. Tell them they will receive a recap of the ideas for further study and refinement. Follow through. This system not only provides new ideas, it has been known to eliminate vexing operational problems as well.

A Way to See Everybody Gets the Word

Pulling in the entire staff for an employee meeting is a costly, difficult task. Yet communications are a vital part of this business. The trouble with most employee meetings is that when one is finally set up, *there is a tendency to try and cover too much material in it*. The important matters that need to be emphasized get obscured by less relevant items. Another factor mitigates against meeting effectiveness: employees that have to be called in for the session are not as receptive to the ideas exchanged as those people already on shift.

☑ *B/L Recommends:* Try a "quickie meeting" program. When something comes up that would normally be an agenda item for some future employee meeting, hold the session immediately. Assemble whoever is on shift and get the topic on the table. *Discuss only that one item.* Limit the meeting time to under ten minutes. Open the meeting by telling employees exactly what is going to be covered. Explain the dimensions of the topic by using a who, what, where, when, why and how structure. Invite questions and comments from the staff. Get the questions out of the way and then summarize everything that was discussed. *Record everything on a tape cassette.* That way, when the rest of the staff comes on shift they can get the word without inconvenience. Your communications will be both consistent and timely. After the entire staff has heard the tape, file it by date and subject. You may wish to issue subsequent printed instructions or use the tape to develop a training manual.

Hermits Have It Made

Hermits never have to be concerned about people disappointing them, not doing what they have been told, not keeping their word, not following through. There is only one problem: Hermits have to do everything by themselves. So, unless you are doing a solo trip you must enter that often misunderstood, underrated, and improperly used people-to-people area called *communication*. How well do you communicate to your assistant or night manager, to your bookkeeper or accounting department, to your purchasing agent or supervisor, to your franchisor, to suppliers, and maintenance people? Up or down the line—to superiors or subordinates—the art of communication is all important.

☑ *B/L Recommends:* Do not just stop at being a good one-to-one communicator. Learn how to express yourself in the written form. There are several excellent and inexpensive books on how to write and string words together so they make sense. You can borrow them at your local library or purchase them in a book store. One good paperback is *The Elements of Style* by William Strunk, Jr. and E. B. White.

One good way to get started is to use simple duplicate "write it once" forms which you can buy from your stationery store. Whenever you ask or tell people to do something important, be sure to write it down for them and yourself. Give or send one copy to the person you want to do something, and keep one copy in your follow-up file. Written memos can sometimes save you a great deal of money. One chain manager we work with successfully defended his actions before a labor review board that questioned the reasons for the dismissal of an employee. He proved the "86" was for just cause. He displayed several copies of handwritten memos of warning he had given the employee prior to termination.

Be brief. Say "please," "thank you." Be specific. Just remember to use the five W's of: Who, What, When, Where, and Why. No longer will you or others have to guess what was told or asked. If you sincerely want to avoid misunderstandings, to be consistent, to be respected as a good leader of people, learn to "write it once" instead of saying it many times. Management people on their way up the ladder of success soon learn that this is one of the very first rungs that must be climbed.

The Green Hornet Strikes . . . Out!

The Green Hornet wanted everybody to like him. The fact that he was in charge of a restaurant grossing over one-half million dollars a year was a matter of considerably less importance. Whenever he had to put a notice or unpopular warning on the bulletin board, he jocularly signed it "The Green Hornet."

That way, he once explained, employees got the warning, but it was good-natured and morale did not suffer. He was wrong on both counts. *Morale did suffer and so did profits*.

The whimsical signature was not the cause. It was a direct indicator of what was the problem with the administration of the store. Like all managers, one of the Hornet's duties was to interpret and implement company policies at store level. The Hornet disliked this aspect of his job. He shunned action whenever he could. When it became absolutely necessary, *the responsibility was put on the shoulders of a fictional character, "The Green Hornet."* Employees quickly became aware of the manager's dilatory approach to decision making. Cliques came into power and the store went downhill. Ultimately, the entire staff and the manager had to be transferred or replaced.

☑ *B/L Recommends:* A lot can be learned about a unit manager's capabilities by just reading his or her bulletin board. *An insecure manager tends to post extra-harsh threats for relatively minor infractions*. He or she will often try to give the message extra force by signing it "the management," instead of using his or her own name. A poor speller, who is aware of this weakness, will sign bulletins with initials only, or not at all, in hope the English miscues will be attributed to somebody else. When a manager signs bulletins with a nom de plume, or something like "You Know Who," *there is a good chance he or she does not like being associated with the contents of the message*. It is a danger signal. On the other hand, a straightforward signature at the bottom of a notice tends to indicate maturity and willingness to lay things on the line.

What Notice on the Bulletin Board?

Have you ever noticed that the size of the employee bulletin board is shrinking? More and more government agencies are demanding that their edicts be placed on employee bulletin boards. As the government takes up more space, *you have to make more effective use of the remaining space*. The bulletin board is still the most inexpensive and practical way to pass the word to employees, but you have to make your messages stand out from the gray haze of government regulations.

☑ *B/L Recommends:* Clean your bulletin board of all old messages. Junk the stuff that is no longer applicable or is not an honest need-to-know bulletin. Rewrite or, preferably, type (double space) memos that are still in effect. Use colored markers to underscore important parts of the memos. Be sure and date each communication. *Leave plenty of room at the bottom of each memo for employee signatures*. Once employees have read and signed the memo, take it down and file it in a three-ring binder. That way, you can bring new employees into the stream by having them read and sign what is in the binder. In the meantime, you have room on the board for new messages.

For the benefit of your non-English speaking staff, see if there is somebody available who can translate your memos. If so, set up a separate display and binder.

What . . . Again?

Employees are saying, "What, again? Another menu increase? When's the boss going to quit raising prices? He's got it made and still wants more. We can't understand it; we just got a new menu less than six months ago." *Operators are saying*, "We must raise prices just to keep pace with rising costs. If we don't, we will go broke."

Employees are unquestionably a foodservice operator's best and first line of defense. Employees can make or break an employer. They can sell anything if they believe in it. They can also cripple an establishment by the display of a poor and insincere attitude if they will not, or cannot, understand what it takes to earn a profit from operations and why their employers are in business.

A REAL PROBLEM: Costs are continuing to go out of sight. A few items have leveled off and stabilized, but others are fast making up for lost time as they spiral upward in cost. Something must be done to counteract these increases.

A BIGGER PROBLEM: Convincing employees that operators are not millionaires, that they deserve and must earn a reasonable return on their time and investment, is imperative—if we are to remain in business. But can and will our personnel understand? Should employees care whether their bosses earn a return on their investments? They have their own problems. Most employees only know that they want more money in their paychecks each year. Few ever think they are being paid what they are worth. And fewer still believe owners are losing money when they see hundreds and thousands of dollars being taken in each day at their cash registers. Incredibly, too many employees believe that their employers are earning over 50 cents of every dollar in net profits.

PERSPECTIVE: Employees are often envious of the managers and owners of their workplaces. They wish they could reverse positions and enjoy the so-called benefits of ownership. They have no idea of what it takes to go into business. Perhaps they have no way to learn. Most employees do not imagine or appreciate the impact of such facts as: an installation cost of over $500 per seat; rents that range into thousands of dollars each month; prices of service plates at over three dollars each; combined wages and food costs ranging from 55 cents to over 70 cents of each dollar taken in gross sales, with a resulting net profit from that dollar of (maybe) 10 cents. Employers are not guaranteed a salary, and most put in well over a 48-hour work week.

COMMUNICATION: It is the fault of the operators that their people do not know or understand their problems. Employees are not going to care unless owners really extend themselves to "show and tell" the facts. Only then will employees begin to realize that their security and future are tied directly to the daily welfare of their employers. *Telling* is not enough. *Showing* is not enough. A start must be made by every operator to truly understand what his or her employees are thinking. They cannot be told what to think. They will think what they want to think if they do not understand *why*.

"Employese" Is a Tough Language to Understand

Workers speak a funny language called "Employese." It sounds like English, *but the words mean different things*. Here's an example: The manager asks a waitress to take care of some minor task. The waitress replies, "I was just going on my break." In English, this response is a trifle obscure. However, anybody fluent in Employese knows this clearly means, "I ain't gonna do it. But, if I have to do it, I'll make the boss feel like the lousy, slave-driving S.O.B. he really is."

☑ *B/L Recommends:* Learn to understand Employese. It will help you construct a more efficient organization. In the above example, the manager had a task that needed doing. After his exchange with the waitress, he was left three choices: (1) Back down and go get somebody else to do the work; (2) Put the job off until the waitress finishes her break; (3) Insist the job be done immediately and risk making the waitress angry. None of these are entirely satisfactory. In Employese, the waitress told the boss something else, and it is important. That is, *the policy on work breaks is not clearly defined*. Had it been, there would have been no need for the exchange.

Informality Breeds Contempt and Aggravation

Mr. Green gets twice as much work accomplished as good old Harry. Yet they are both the same person. When friendly, unassuming Harry Green was promoted to manager, he tacitly approved the use of first names for everybody in the house. Nothing like working with one big family, right? As the house's top man, *he soon found out this kind of informality exacts a stiff price in day-to-day aggravation*. As good old Harry, he had a problem moving salespeople out of his office. Drummers didn't think Harry could say no and make it stick. The delivery people treated him with about the same good humored contempt they gave the buspersons. Handling customer gripes as Harry, the manager, didn't work either. He couldn't settle employee disputes without taking a lot of flack from all contending parties. Inevitably, the work started to suffer. The employees thought they had a friend. *Here he was, some of the time, acting like a boss*. When one of the hostesses yelled across the packed dining room, "Harry, there's some broad on the phone for you," Mr. Green took charge of the restaurant. Mr. Green gets a lot of things done with a lot less effort.

☑ *B/L Recommends:* Managers: insist on the formal method of address. After all, *a manager is running a formal business and not a family reunion*. Things work better when the person who has to call the shots demands and gets the respect the position deserves.

Cross My Heart and Hope to Die

Promises made by management regarding future rewards for today's inconveniences are obligations to be honored. Employees' promises are also obligations. We've all heard such statements as "Let me off early and I'll work the next holiday," and "If I can have an advance on my pay I'll buy an alarm clock and never be late again." Any experienced operator can supply a list of a hundred or more similar promises.

☑ *B/L Recommends: A promise is like a debt, except that it's an obligation of character, not cash.* When management accepts a promise in exchange for a favor or an unearned benefit, it would be foolish to permit the debtor to escape without paying. Every obligation must be paid, and every debt must be collected without fail. That way, promises will only be given by those who are willing to pay off.

The Third Degree

Criminals know that if caught they must answer a barrage of questions and have the correct answers—or else. They cannot expect robbery or murder to be forgiven with a few "I'm sorry's," or "I just felt like it." *Absenteeism is a crime against both the house and the guest, and should not be excused lightly.* What sort of attitude do your people have concerning absence or tardiness? Do your employees know how to test you and selectively take off a day or two each month? Do they teach new employees all the tricks?

☑ *B/L Recommends: Let your employees know you are watching.* Stress that good attendance is a "must" from their first interview. Require that employees call in if absent, and call them back to check on their condition, advise of any shift changes, and to determine if they will be healthy enough to pull their regular shift the next day. Do not accept feeble excuses. One operator we know reduced his absenteeism rate by posting the names of his employees with absence and tardiness checks and perfect attendance records. Employees may see it as one thing to let the boss down, but a different situation when they are shown letting their fellow crew members down.

Give Yourself a Call, Sometime

It may sound crazy, but you can learn a lot about your standing in the community by calling your restaurant, or listening on the extension when someone else calls. *Telephone etiquette is a part of your restaurant's image,* and poor telephone manners can turn customers away. Frequently the person answering the phone will give out such information as "The owner is never here on Tuesdays," or "He's always gone in the afternoon." Whether true or not, your schedule is your business, not that of a con artist or robber.

☑ *B/L Recommends:* Communication is the foundation of business. The telephone is communication, pure and simple. *An employee's use of the telephone on your behalf is as much subject to your rules and standards as their personal conduct in the presence of the customer*—perhaps more so, because the words and the inflection and the voice are all the customer has to go by.

Help Waitresses Be Calm, Cool—and Collect

At the end of the rush period, one waitress looks calm and tidy. The one handling the station right beside her looks like she has barely survived a major earthquake. Why? The reasons range from psychological to physical with a lot of complex combinations in between. What is there to do?

☑ *B/L Recommends:* Make it a point to check waiters and waitresses as the rush period slows down. Customers dislike being served by disheveled, unorganized personnel. When a waiter or waitress looks messy, it is an indication he or she is having trouble handling the station. It could be poor training, attitude, or simply that he or she is trying to handle too many tasks at one time. *Discuss job requirements with the serving person*. Explain how an untidy appearance or tense expression affects tips. Advise against bringing at-home problems to work. If necessary, make changes in the service pattern. Place full-length mirrors in the back end so serving personnel can check their appearance before going on the floor, and get a look at themselves as they come off rush periods. Help personnel to take pride in the way they look; it translates to more money for them, and increased business for the restaurant.

In Recognition of . . .

Everybody's used to seeing name tags on the serving personnel, the cashiers, and sometimes, the service assistants. Who provides recognition for the cooks? One large national chain does, with a large reader-board on the passbar. Cooks coming on shift hang their nameplates on the board, and take them down when they leave. *One large restaurant in Los Angeles has a spot on the menu for "Chef Smith's Specialty."* One extremely popular resort in northern California places tent cards on the tables, stating, "Your waitress' name is Mary Jones."

☑ *B/L Recommends:* Employees are individuals; they need and deserve recognition. They are not cogs in a machine. Employees have talents and abilities an employer never sees if he or she concentrates on creating a plastic palace just like the one down the street. It is the character, individuality, and personality of the employees that gives character and individuality to a restaurant. *If character and individuality are scare words, perhaps your plates should be delivered on a conveyor belt*.

The "Ghostess" Will Seat Your Party

During rush periods, a restaurant pays a very high price for its phone service. When a host or hostess is on the phone instead of the floor seating customers, the call can *cost an average coffee shop anywhere from $5.00 to $35.00 a minute*. When a hostess is on the phone, there is a "ghostess" on the floor.

☑ *B/L Recommends: Study the pattern of incoming calls.* Do not permit the host or hostess to get tied up with frivolous phone calls during peak business periods. He or she should not be expected to screen the manager's calls, answer job inquiries, or arrange employment interviews during the rush.

The Cook on Watch Is the Cook to Watch

It is unfair to describe some galley installations in new restaurants as hell-holes. Most good hell-holes are not that hot or cramped. In a frenetic desire to maximize tabletops in the front end, designers keep chiseling away kitchen work areas. In theory, more tabletops are supposed to produce more profit. However, *the decisive factor is the product that goes on the tabletops*. A difficult work area makes it tough to maintain quality control. When quality control goes, so do the customers.

A client recently told us he had looked everywhere trying to locate the reason for a prolonged volume slump. He checked store procedures, menu pricing, labor turnover, area income level, competition and even his advertising budget. No clues were forthcoming. He should have taken a good look at his cooks, particularly near the end of a shift. The galley was tough to work. On top of that, cooks were being allowed to double-shift at their own discretion. It was the kind of situation where the element of survival takes priority over cuisine. Additionally, nobody had counseled the cooks on the hazards of attempting to replace depleted body fluids with alcohol. The irrational behavior and tantrums caused by this oversight were merely regarded as little idiosyncrasies that go with the craft. Waiters and waitresses had to tolerate the situation, customers did not.

☑ *B/L Recommends: Learn to look for signs that indicate a cook is asking for help.* Pride in their own ability to work in mean situations makes it hard for most cooks to verbalize their needs. The signs of incipient exhaustion, alcoholism, or drug use are recognizable. Public libraries have extensive material on these symptoms. When the indicators show up, immediate corrective action is necessary. This can range from personal counseling, to better labor scheduling, to reorganization of the equipment layout. To watch quality control, you have to watch the cook.

Incentive Reviews Are a Must

It used to be called a "working wage." Then the politicians got into it and it became a minimum wage. Now we have something that can best be defined as "breathing pay." If an employee can inhale and exhale reasonably well and get to work on time, his or her future is pretty well assured by federal fiat. The pay, hiring, firing, and working conditions are strictly regulated the same as in any government bureau. When an agency is subsidized, this works fine. Unfortunately, a restaurant is not a tax subsidized activity. It has to depend on a high order of efficiency to produce profits. Attempting to turn a profit or even stay in business under regulations notorious for producing waste and inefficiency is a formidable challenge. The only way it can be overcome is by maintaining peak efficiency. This means attracting, training, motivating, and retaining individuals willing to give some perspiration in addition to respiration.

☑ *B/L Recommends:* Review and realign your pay incentive program to compensate for new minimum wage escalations. Do not abandon incentive increases; just be very cautious in awarding them. *Employees, good or bad, are more valuable than ever,* if only because the government says you have to pay more for them. Efficient employees require recognition and compensation beyond government decreed levels. Otherwise, they will vanish through that swinging door along with the "breathers." However, *impulsively awarding pay hikes is a hazardous practice.* Your incentive program has to be planned and set to take into account "Uncle's" long-term demands. Make sure employees are aware of this very important fact of business life.

There are other motivational techniques that can be used to supplement wage increases. They take careful handling. They require adequate thought and preparation. In the past five years, a great deal of expensive research has been conducted in the motivation area. Most collegiate and public libraries have good contemporary texts on the subject. Review what they have to offer. A few hours' study may provide you with the basics of a program that can maintain high productivity without entailing debilitating expense.

SECURITY,
LARCENY, AND PILFERAGE

Better to put a strong fence
around the cliff
than an ambulance
down in the valley.

4

SECURITY, LARCENY, AND PILFERAGE

Security experts claim there are some four thousand ways that employees can steal from you. Believe them! However, you cannot spend all your waking hours defending yourself against those who would cheat you of your hard-earned goods and money.

This section deals with some of the obvious and many of the subtle ways that you can lose your valuable customers, personnel, merchandise, and profits. Your best defenses are your knowledge, communications, documentation, and the willingness to approach this vital subject maturely and professionally to reduce the opportunities and climate for such dastardly acts against you and your business.

Gone with the Wind

Well, not quite. Pictures, wall decor, planters, and other attractive or useful items often disappear from our restaurants by *hand*—not by the wind. This type of pilferage, usually by customers, is widespread. No operation is pilfer-proof. Few establishments can escape being ripped off from time to time.

☑ ***B/L Recommends:*** Literally tie down whatever items you can which are within easy reach of your guests. Decorative items near exits partially obscured from view are prime targets for customers who may want to take mementos of their visit to your place. Tack or screw down picture frames and wall decor. Restroom items are particularly susceptible. Metal toilet tissue holder rollers, sink stoppers, hardware, and even light bulbs turn up among the missing. Unquestionably, these events and our eventual mistrust of "guests" can embitter us if we allow them to color our thinking. Most professionals do all they can to protect themselves, as we have suggested. They consider such losses a pain in their pocketbooks, but nevertheless an integral part of their operating expenses.

Walkouts Are an Unendangered Species

There is a lower form of animal life which we would love to see hit the endangered species list—walkouts. Unfortunately, the breed seems to be growing and multiplying. *One reason: Temptation is greater due to higher meal prices.* There is almost no penalty involved, other than minor embarrassment, when one of these animals is trapped. Yet not all walkouts come about through criminal intent. Sometimes the individual is expressing his or her dissatisfaction with the food, service, or both.

☑ *B/L Recommends: Avoid working short on the floor.* Walkouts are a real threat when this happens. Keep serving personnel actively supervising the tables on their stations. Unobstructed visibility in the dining room and cashstand area act as a deterrent to walkouts. Above all, *make it quick and simple for the customers to pay their tabs.* They will not wait at the cashstand forever when the exit is just a few tempting feet away.

Ha Ha, You Can't Use It Anymore

Sounds a bit like what our little sisters or brothers used to say when they were envious about something we had which they did not. Remember how children break or tear things often for no real reason? Their response when questioned may be "just because." Unfortunately, many of our customers (children of all ages) have yet to grow up. They like to destroy perfectly good foods—"just because." Guests often believe that every bit of food—condiments, breads, butter, rolls, crackers, jellies, sugar, etc.—placed in front of them *belongs only to them!* And if they do not, or cannot, use these table foods they either take them, or worse—*destroy them.* Haven't you seen such evidence as mashed butter chips, broken crackers, crushed breads, pierced jelly packets, and ketchup smeared into the mustard—all literally destroyed so no one can use them?

☑ *B/L Recommends:* Train your help to remove your table foods as soon as it becomes apparent they are no longer needed to make a meal an enjoyable experience. Teach them to be alert for the sake of your cost of sales as well as the comfort of your guests. Foods should never be destroyed unless they are unfit to be served. It makes little difference as to the type of establishment you operate. Customers who may be nuts or playful will take a shot at anything on their table or counter to destroy, mess up, or break. Discuss this point with your service personnel. Teach them that their explanation to their customers should be that they wish to make room for the entrees. They should ask if they might remove the items that are apparently no longer needed, and should remove all table foods along with the dirty dishes, as soon as possible.

Those Murderous Handguns

The owner of a fast food outlet was the victim of a stickup. The next day he brought a handgun into his store for self-protection. He will never be held up again. Four nights after the incident, he heard a commotion out in front of the store. He grabbed his pistol and went out to take a look. *The cops gunned him down.* It was a tragic mixup. Regardless who holds them, handguns are lethal.

☑ *B/L Recommends: Keep guns out of the store.* Sure, circumstances occur that make a manager sometimes wish he or she had a gun. But it is better to be able to wish than to be dead.

The Good News Can Be Bad News

The cops got lucky. They caught the two holdup men a block away from the hot dog stand. The owner of the stand had installed a silent alarm. The police deserved some credit. They had answered swiftly before on three false alarms risking lives and patrol cares. But when they announced this triumph of law and order over the forces of darkness and evil, the cops told the press that the holdup occurred on a Tuesday afternoon, the take was $360, and it was from the cash register. *No doubt the alarm system will get another test.*

☑ *B/L Recommends:* The police like to present a good image, just like everybody else. Generally, they will respect your views following a robbery loss. Therefore, *tell them you do not want dollar amounts, time, place, and day announced after a stickup occurs, regardless of the outcome.* The guys that hold up stores can usually read. You do not need this type of want ad in the public press. The history of this store, from the standpoint of security, is bad. That's why the owner went to the expense of a silent alarm.

Employees, the cops, even the stickup guys who cased the place and saw the money and not the alarm, would have been less endangered if cash deposit discipline had been enforced. What can you say good about a hot dog stand that has $360 in the till after the noon rush is over? The place treats its food well, too bad they don't give the same consideration to cash received and the safety of employees.

Hold Out on Holdup Information

Just about everybody has written instructions on what to do when there is a holdup in the store. The instructions all read pretty much the same, since most of them were originated by the insurance companies. It is not difficult to figure out who they are trying to protect the most. We have no quarrel with the procedures suggested. *However, most instructions leave out a very important point.* They do not firmly caution employees against the hazards of talking about store security arrangements and emergency procedures. Not long ago, a newspaper article quoted a store manager as saying that all his people knew exactly what to do if a holdup occurred: "Give up the money quick!" Up to that point, his store had never been hit. Right after the story appeared, it was. Whether it is for business or a stickup, when you advertise for customers, you generally get them.

☑ *B/L Recommends: Don't be helpful to stickup artists.* Review your emergency procedures. Be sure employees and managers are fully warned, in print and at meetings, on the dangers of discussing company procedures. Most holdup artists only move when they think they have a sure thing going for themselves.

You and Your Big Mouth

Ever stop to think that you may be talking too much? Is it possible that you, who are responsible for the complete business of your store, may actually be divulging classified information to both insiders and outsiders? You may be placing your establishment and people in jeopardy by inviting a holdup, or break-in. Too often have we seen cashiers, managers, assistants, and hostesses advertise how much money is in the house when taking cash from customers as they report confidential tape readings to owners, supervisors, book-keepers, and others over the telephone.

☑ *B/L Recommends:* Do not *publicly* announce your daily cash register readings. Many make a game of beating yesterday's, last week's, or last month's totals. It is nice to have the old company spirit. We raise no objection to it. But to advertise these facts too enthusiastically to all who may be listening can lead to devastating results. Believe us. Other casual conversations that contain tip-off information such as rear safes or registers being broken, having two or three deposits still in the house, might be the tip someone's been waiting to hear and/or pass on to someone else. Loose lips could sink your ship. Play it cool.

Holdup on Your Bulletin Board

"In the Event of a Robbery . . ." is a bulletin board notice which we have produced as part of a management training course on restaurant security. The Los Angeles Police Department hands out these notices to retailers attending their robbery prevention seminars.

☑ *B/L Recommends:* If you do not already have similar instructions posted on your bulletin board, you can now. *It is our fervent hope that your staff will never have to use the information.* But being prepared is the best way to wet down any emergency.

In the Event of a Robbery . . .

There is a possibility that a criminal may some day select this business as the target for a holdup. For this reason, we are posting this notice to provide guidelines for the behavior of employees who might be present.

FIRST . . .

You are expected to cooperate in every way with an armed robber. Any person committing an armed robbery is bound to be under great tension. No crew member should do or say anything that will increase that tension.

SECOND . . .

You are expected to give up any cash or supplies that the criminal demands. There should be no resistance, no attempt to deceive the criminal concerning the amount or location of what he or she asks for. At the same time, no information should be volunteered.

THIRD . . .

You are expected to carefully observe all physical characteristics of the criminal so that they can later be relayed to the police who investigate the robbery.

FOURTH . . .

After the criminal has departed, each witness should write down all the facts that can be remembered. Each person should write without consulting others who are present. When questioned by the police, full and complete cooperation should be given so they can catch the criminal.

Descriptions and the written summary of the incident should be based on the following outline, which may be used as a guide.

What was the criminal's height?

Look straight into the criminal's eyes. If the eyes are above yours, he or she is taller; if the eyes are below yours, the criminal is shorter. Estimate how many inches taller or shorter.

What was the color of the criminal's eyes?

When looking into the criminal's eyes to gauge height, look at the color. This is very difficult to disguise.

What was the color of the criminal's skin?

Even a masked criminal will have exposed skin around the eyes, hands, or around the collar.

What was the criminal's weight or body type?

You may have trouble estimating what a person weighs, but in describing the criminal to the police, you can compare him or her to another employee, or a member of the police. You would say, "The criminal was built like that person, but slightly heavier."

How would you describe the criminal's voice?

A voice would, first of all, be male or female. Then, it would be high-pitched or low. The criminal would speak slowly or rapidly. Did he or she speak with an accent, such as a foreign accent, a Boston accent, or a Texas accent?

Was the criminal right- or left-handed?

The criminal will probably carry the weapon in the hand he or she favors. Remember which hand it was, and whether he or she switched hands to perform some other act.

How was the criminal dressed?

Look at each item of clothing from top to bottom. Did the criminal wear a hat?—what kind and what color? Did he or she wear a coat?—what kind and what color? Shirt? Sweater? A belt with an unusual buckle? What kind of pants? What color? What kind of shoes? What color?

How did the criminal leave, and which way did he or she go?

DON'T follow the criminal outside when he or she leaves. Look through the window. Try to get the make, model, and color of the car. Get the license number if possible. Notice which way he or she turned into the street.

Key Man Insurance

Even though they are made of metal, keys have a distressing tendency to "float." That's just one problem. *Left unguarded, door, alarm, and storeroom keys can reproduce themselves like rabbits.* Turning keys over to a cleaning service is risky. Keeping alarm and door keys on the same ring as car keys is a bad policy. The cleaning service and auto shop no doubt have honest owners, but this does not certify all their employees. In shady bars and poolrooms around the country, keys can be purchased like popcorn.

☑ *B/L Recommends:* Periodically changing lock combinations and keys is as practical as repairing a leaky roof, and is done for the same reason: It keeps out unwanted elements. Virtually every piece of merchandise in your store has a value to someone. *We have encouraged operators to try to do cleaning and maintenance work with in-house personnel during business hours*. If you must use outside services, insist they service your unit at specified hours when you have responsible people available to keep an eye on the vendor's crew.

Beware of Telephone Con Artists

The names, telephone numbers, and addresses of your employees are valuable. Not just to you, but to union organizers, as well as people who market spurious merchandise and services. They use high-pressure telephone sales tactics to get the information. They imply that the information is needed for prizes or discounts or for legal matters—*never the real purpose*. Con artists are successful because they are able to contact unwary people who want to be helpful, like service personnel and hosts or hostesses.

☑ *B/L Recommends:* Employee names and addresses should be maintained in a locked confidential file. Regardless of how legitimate the caller may sound, no business or personnel information should be given over the phone except on a call back. Before calling back, *check the phone book to see if the company or government agency actually exists*. Call the phone book number first to find out whether you are actually dealing with an authorized representative.

The Old Scam Has a New Twist

The invoice is stamped "Second Notice." It is a photo copy of what seems to be an original invoice for repair services performed more than sixty days ago. *What happened to the first invoice is a mystery*. That long ago, nobody can even remember who ordered the work done. Under the circumstances, probably the best thing to do is mail payment to the post office box designated on the invoice.

☑ *B/L Recommends:* Do not do any of the above. You will be contributing to another swindle making the rounds. It's a dressed up version of the old phony advertising gimmick. The key, of course, is the post office box address and failure to show a phone number. *When in doubt, don't pay*.

Watch Out for Those Phantom Suppliers

In the restaurant business, there is a reason for everything. There is a reason for operational expenses to be four percent higher than they should. There is also a reason why the cause is sometimes difficult to detect. Working with a full service operation recently, we rewrote procedures, re-trained people and kept our fingers on the pulse of the business for six weeks. To our chagrin, the expense figures still came in higher than they should have. We reviewed the entire operational setup. Everything checked out. That left only one place to look. The owner employed an outside accountant. The owner not only placed complete trust in the accountant, he placed all the checkbooks in his hands as well. The accountant had worked for him for years, the owner told us. *The phantom suppliers the accountant was writing checks for may have been around almost as long.* We don't know, the accountant was allowed to scrap the invoices at his own discretion.

We rarely encounter shifty accountants. This is a danger in itself. Owners place such complete trust in these people that they seldom question anything the accountant says. Last summer, a dinnerhouse operator we know took a European vacation. He left the country thinking he had $90,000 in the bank. He actually had about half that, but he took the word of his bookkeeper. When he returned, he was broke. The bookkeeper had been siphoning funds from the checking account to make up for stock market losses. The pressure got to be too much; the bookkeeper cleaned out the rest of the account and left on his own vacation to South America.

☑ **B/L Recommends:** If operational expenses are out of line and you cannot find the reason, *start signing your own checks*. Be especially careful about invoices for services, flue cleaning, roof repairs, janitorial services and landscaping. Fake invoices are cheap to print. When they are for services rendered, they do not flash warning signals in the area of food and labor costs. There is always the possibility of supplier collusion, particularly with small companies. But you know what your costs should be. If you are controlling your checks, it is a simple matter to pick up the phone and dial the telephone number on an invoice before you pick up your pen.

Time Cards, Labor Schedules, Employment Applications

There are not only some "phantom suppliers" around; "phantom employees" are a hazard as well. This is particularly true in operations with absentee management, and in chain organizations utilizing centralized payroll preparation. We constantly advise clients: *Time card security is important*. Time cards should never be issued indiscriminately. A time card is only a piece of cardboard until it is filled in. But when it is completed, it constitutes a demand for payment almost as authoritative as a bank check. You do not issue bank checks frivolously, don't do it with time cards.

Let's take a look at the life cycle of a phantom employee. The proud parent is usually an unsupervised and unscrupulous night manager or assistant manager. Or the parent may be the manager of a satellite unit located some distance from the chain's home office. He or she completes the forms necessary to enter a new employee on the payroll. These materials go into the payroll office, where, among all the other new-hires, it causes no concern. The phantom employee has been born. Daddy, the crooked manager, puts the kid right to work by forwarding a completed time card every week. *He takes custody of the returned payroll check, cashes it through the register and pockets the money.*

There is some small risk involved while the scam is in operation. But once the employee is terminated, the possibility of being caught is just about gone forever. So the manager usually knocks the kid off in four or five weeks by sending in a termination notice. If everything goes smoothly, he'll create another phantom employee the following month. As everyone knows, new employees do not grasp regulations too well. Thus, any embarrassing or suspicious questions from the home office can be answered quickly and simply by terminating the latest phantom on the payroll.

Unless proper controls are in effect, the amount of money a devious manager can make with phantom hiring and firing is really only limited by how many points of labor he can hide in the profit and loss statement. He can also cut into the schedule and service and not raise the labor figure at all.

☑ *B/L Recommends:* Original employment applications should be filed at the payroll preparation source. If store copies are necessary, they can be photocopied by the manager before they are submitted. If in doubt about the status of a new employee, send a first class postage address verification letter to the employee's home address. Ask the employee to sign the verification and return it in your postage-paid return envelope. *If the letter itself is returned due to a bad address, something is wrong.* From time to time, supervisors should personally pay the employees of the units under their jurisdiction. That way, the supervisor sees every person who claims a check and discovers when there is an extra unclaimed check.

Require that labor schedules be prepared on a schedule form. Do not permit managers to prepare schedules on placemats or shopping bags from the supermarket. Schedules should be prepared using the employee's last name, first name, and initial, instead of "Joe," "Pete," "Mary," and so on. You need a schedule that can be lined up with the payroll journal for verification purposes. If you link time cards, labor schedules, employment applications together as a control system, you can eliminate the phantom employee menace. You may not have the problem now, but if a phantom can get into your work force, it is almost a cinch that sooner or later he will.

A Taxing Situation for Management

We recently sat in on a hiring session for a new restaurant. In the course of several interviews, we uncovered a rather unusual scam. The waitress being interviewed asked with innocent directness, *how much we intended to pad the sales tax.* We had no answer for that question. She said that in her last job, the manager required that the sales tax be padded a penny or two on all checks over two dollars. This petty graft probably contributed about seventy dollars a week to the manager's own retirement fund.

☑ *B/L Recommends:* Aside from the fact this is a clear-cut case of coercion, it shows what happens when managers are permitted to package their own fringe benefits. *Company guest check audits would have prevented the problem.*

This You Won't Believe—Unless You've Had Experience!

Innocent managers in this tough "street-smart" business cannot believe that their people will steal from them. New operators feel that they are such fine leaders that their employees will be dedicated, loyal, ethical, absolutely honest, and never take advantage of their position to take anything away from them. Correct? Unfortunately, we are too gullible at first. Later on many of us become too hardened, but still are unable to cope with such dishonesty and disloyalty, because we never developed sufficient disciplines and controls.

Security experts claim that 82 percent of all employees will steal from their employers. Certainly the degree of pilferage will vary from one extreme to the other. Owners and managers in every foodservice operation suffer from higher food costs and operating expenses because of internal pilferage. Personnel who feel they are not fully appreciated for what they do, all too frequently rationalize that it's okay to "borrow" things from their bosses as a form of further compensation. To others the taking, or giving, of "free" merchandise is just a game to play against those in authority. Employees do not realize how crippling excessive losses from internal thievery can be to a foodservice operation.

☑ *B/L Recommends:* You must *take a positive approach to the subject of pilferage and theft with all personnel from their very first day on the job.* Explain fully the meaning of pilferage and what losses can do to threaten the job security of every employee and the future of the operation itself. Show everyone that you know what it's all about. Start each person off with the knowledge that your systems and procedures have a definite meaning. Don't hush-hush the subject and think it will go away. Do not dare them to steal! Do not create a challenge! And do not tolerate excessive shortages of money from your daily receipts. Check and double-check every minor loss of merchandise and money. Be constructively upset. Pull frequent cash register tape readings and inventories. Instruct that everything has and must be kept in its proper place. Involve your crew in your thorough effort to reduce and eliminate unexplained losses. Avoid bringing this serious problem out into the open and you will add to the frightening statistic that 82 percent of *your* employees steal!

Let's See . . . That's Three People Times $5.00 Per Shift?

You do not have to be an Einstein to compute the answer to this problem. One of our secretary-typists told us of her former employment with a franchisee of a national ice cream company. She had just completed some work for us regarding rip-offs and internal pilferage. She was not surprised that we knew of such goings-on. It was the extent and frequency that bothered her. She had worked steadily for this franchisee for over a year while still in high school. Naturally, her friends came by frequently to say hello. She said it was not unusual for her and the other two or three employees to give away some five dollars in free goodies to their friends each evening. And to top it off, they all took home one to two quarts of ice cream "free of charge" each evening. You can mentally add up the tremendous losses this operator must have incurred. We are willing to bet his company supervisor must have cautioned him time and again about over-scooping and portion control, but never once got to the source of the problem.

☑ *B/L* **Recommends:** *Do not believe your people to be incapable of pilferage!* This young lady did not consider herself to be a thief. She was just being *friendly.* Her friends expected her to give a little. A cone here, a hot fudge sundae there, did not seem that much to her. No one seemed to care or say anything about free, unaccounted give-aways. She remembers being told about waste, over-scooping, temperature, cleanliness, and customer awareness. But, she was never told about the giving or taking of ice cream without charge. We checked the Manual of Operations of this franchisor just to see if it contained any reference to this serious and ever-present problem. We could not find one word about it! Apparently this national chain decided to hush-hush this subject and not even refer or admit to its existence. The franchisee therefore was left on his own to learn the hard way. Franchisors are supposed to pre-think and advise of problem areas for their franchisees.

You must attack this problem head-on. Our young lady said *she would have reacted positively* to any constructive reprimands and explanations of how her acts of pilferage were detrimental to the cost-of-sales and profits of her employer—had she been told! Q.E.D., she was not told—so she did not know.

Cost Controls Need Constant Attention

It is difficult to give away food and still make a profit. As basic as that point is, we frequently spend a lot of time and effort proving it to clients. In the latest instance, a 15-year-old coffee shop had good consistent volume, but profits were suddenly falling off. The store's cost control systems were average; they had not changed appreciably since the store first opened. There was nothing in the records to show why the store was buying so much food and realizing so little profit.

The source of the problem, we found, was three years in the making. At about that time, the restaurant experimented with an all-you-can-eat promotion. It was a big hit with the customers. Management decided to increase the number of nights it was available, and also the variety of dishes featured. The promotion became a standard attraction. Somewhere along the line, waitresses got tired of writing "re-order" on the guest checks. *They simply started calling "re" at the fry station window.* This worked all right as long as everybody played honest. About the time profits started to slide, an unscrupulous waitress joined the staff. She quickly realized what potential there was in being able to get food out of the fry station without a written order. That's when she began selling the restaurant's food at her station at a very substantial discount. She was calling a half-dozen "re's" for every ticket she was writing. The cooks quickly caught on to what was happening. Instead of blowing the whistle, they started carrying home some fringe benefits of their own. Since the items being skimmed were confined to the all-you-can-eat specials, it was hard to pinpoint the source of the losses.

☑ *B/L Recommends:* Review your cost control systems. Are they being fully complied with by all personnel? Even the most insignificant breach of a system can mean a loss of thousands of dollars. In the above incident, *there was no dishonest intent when the system was first broken*. For months it ticked along—like a time bomb. When the real trouble started, the thefts were masked by a long-established and accepted pattern of doing business.

The Cigar and Candy Caper

Ever notice the number of maintenance people that have a penchant for smoking fine cigars? *You would too, if you got them for free.* Cashstand candies are no doubt responsible for putting more holes in the teeth of waitress' kids than the combined forces of bubble gum and soda pop. These unintended fringe benefits make it tough to produce a profit and loss statement that truly reflects a picture of the business.

☑ *B/L Recommends:* Despite the blandishments of specialty candy sellers, it's next to impossible to profit by selling candy at the cashstand. *Don't try.* If you want to make mints available, list them as a promotional expense. Even when the house manager doesn't smoke cigars, they often get ignored at inventory time. From a management standpoint, nothing goes better with a good cigar than a locked display case.

Keep That Storeroom Locked

An open storeroom invites pilferage. Pilferage drives up your food cost. But we know that cooks and other crew members will complain that they can't get the food and supplies needed to work with when management is not available to unlock the storeroom.

☑ *B/L Recommends:* Build a shelf in the back of the restaurant and place on it one can or package of each item that might be needed. When management returns, or first thing in the morning, usage can be seen at once and compared to volume. We have seen this simple method lower food costs in many restaurants.

"One Mistake Coming Up!"

Said the dishwasher to the fountain man, "Make me a chocolate hot fudge sundae *mistake,* will ya?" "*Burn* a steak for me when I take my break," said the waitress to the cook. "Save the *extra* malts for me," said the busperson to the waitress. "*Crush* me a piece of apple pie," said the cook to the waitress. Mistakes will happen. Foods, beverages, and desserts will on occasion be improperly prepared, burned, over-cooked, or messed up beyond recognition. Items that are not up-to-spec should not be served to your guests. However, what of the "accidents" that are not honest mistakes but, *on purpose?*

☑ *B/L Recommends:* Beware! The more strict you are about which foods your personnel are allowed to eat, the greater may be their "errors." It is natural for your people to believe that it would be a shame to "86" good, edible food. This justifies their actions as they go to extremes creating gastronomical goodies for each other all in the name of a *mistake*. Your present food cost is probably taking a beating. You must step in and stop this practice from getting out of hand. You cannot forbid mistakes, but you can instruct they be recorded on a guest check or employee ticket. You must let your employees know you are aware of this game carried on against your system of procedures.

Foodstuffs are not to be played with, destroyed on purpose, or otherwise manipulated for any purpose other than to benefit your guests. Let it be known that unauthorized mi*steaks* are expensive and will not be tolerated.

Oops, It Was a Little Mistake, or Was It?

To err is human. To forgive can sometimes be dumb. Waiters, waitresses, and counter people who write up orders will make mistakes. Customers will change their minds and request other foods and beverages. The written orders have to be voided, erased, crossed out, or altered in some fashion. *Do you have a set procedure for making guest check corrections?* Sometimes mistakes can be intentional.

☑ *B/L Recommends:* Require service personnel to have any guest check changes initialed by the senior person on the floor. Employees have been known to run their own discount operation. They write the ticket correctly, then after the food is served to a friend, they alter the total and put in a low price. Be firm. Maintain a strict policy that at least *two persons must be involved when a guest check correction is required.*

Grrreat—Your Books Balanced Out Again!

Day in, or rather, *night in and night out* your cash-on-hand balances perfectly with your cash register tape readings. To the penny, there are no shortages or overages. You are understandably pleased. You really believe you have a right to take pride in the fact that your personnel are so perfect.

☑ *B/L Recommends:* Do not be quite so darn pleased. Most cashiers, cash handlers, service personnel, assistants, and night managers are just *not that accurate*. There are usually just too many people who have access to your cash in the course of a day who may make mistakes. A few cents off, a buck short or over, is more believable. Overages and shortages are as normal as blueberry pie. Stores that even out to the penny (almost) every night just might be giving the signal that there may be some hanky-panky going on.

We have investigated many accounts to find closing and opening crews having played games with client monies such as: using overages to balance out shortages; taking money from their own pockets to make up shortages, then on other occasions taking overages to replace more than what they previously gave. Others have lost tapes on purpose. Many have written up false overrings and faked paid-outs to balance their books in order to take valuable dollars from their employers. Others have been known to purposely foul up their cash registers to cover losses and thefts of cash. A perfect set of books each day is desirable, but with any great frequency, unlikely. Demonstrate to yourself whether this statement is reasonably true. Work closing and opening shifts, and check the money handling and closing routines. Watch for a pattern to develop. You may be able to pinpoint those who are fooling around with your money.

A Calculated Answer to Undercharging

We thought our new client was overreacting to the problem he was having with undercharges. He gave up admonishing waitresses on a daily basis. *He went out and bought them all pocket calculators.* It seemed like a rather costly way to solve the dilemma at the time. Actually, it has worked out quite well. He eliminated undercharges. The serving personnel enjoy the ease and convenience the number machines provide. Customers appreciate the extra touch of thoroughness. Disputes and questions about guest check entries have been greatly reduced.

☑ *B/L Recommends:* If you are being plagued with undercharges, *consider issuing calculators*. Regardless of how much you teach, preach, beg, or scream about the subject, it persists. Employees have an entrenched belief that it is your money, not theirs, that is being lost. When they get busy, they are simply not as careful with guest check addition as they should be.

If you go the calculator route, set up a battery recharging system. Either check the calculators in an out with each shift, or collect a deposit for the item as you do for uniforms.

Quick Count for Guest Checks

Most restaurants require waiters and waitresses to sort completed checks back into numerical order before turning them in to the owner. Few owners bother to check to see that all the checks are returned. There is a quick and easy method to make sure check books are complete.

☑ *B/L Recommends:* Before issuing a new book of checks, use a broad felt-tip marking pen (one-fourth inch wide) to draw a diagonal line from top to bottom on one edge of all the checks in the book. When the book is complete, the line goes smoothly from top to bottom. When a check is missing or out of sequence, the line jumps, indicating a break in the numbers.

Cleanup Eliminates Cover-up at Night

It was not the store's owner that showed the night crew members the error of their ways. *It was a rapist*. The crew had started playing the old "cover-up" game. When things were slow, two of the three people on the night shift would take off early. The last one, whose turn it was, would shut down early and hang around until it was time to clock everyone out. When the criminal saw there was only one car in the parking lot and the store was closed, he simply hung around until the waitress came out of the door. He forced her back inside and some very unpleasant things transpired. If the crew had been on the job *instead of stealing wages,* the atrocity probably would not have taken place. Apologies are no substitute for common sense.

☑ *B/L Recommends:* Warn everybody about the danger of playing "cover-up" at night. If you cannot check back periodically late at night, there is another thing that can be done to maintain job discipline. Leave the night crew a long list of cleaning chores that must be completed. If the crew is too busy to do the work, the cash register tape will indicate the fact. Workers will not be anxious to cover for each other if it means the person left behind has to do the cleanup work for three people. *Keeping them busy keeps them safe, and you get a cleaner store in the bargain.*

This Really Was a Smashing Promotion

They had a smash grand opening at the new sandwich and ice cream parlor. We hope the grand re-opening will be less spectacular. The owners of the store thought it would be a clever idea to give away silk-screened T-shirts to the first one hundred customers through the door on opening day. When they told us of the plan, we said it was a lousy idea. But the ads and the shirts were already ordered; they felt they had to go ahead with the promotion.

We advised the owners to talk over their plans with the watch commander at the police station. *They forgot*. On grand opening morning, a Saturday, about four hundred teenagers were on hand before the doors opened. The jostling and shoving to get up front turned into a fist-swinging riot.

The cops were taken by surprise. *Saturday morning riot calls are rare* and this was normally a quiet neighborhood. Considerable damage was done to the premises before police got things under control. Fortunately, there were no serious physical injuries. Nonetheless, parents, police, shopping center management, and the insurance carriers are pretty ticked off. The store faces a precarious future.

☑ *B/L Recommends:* If you have an event scheduled that is likely to draw a large crowd, always check in with the local police. They probably will not give you much encouragement. Their job is to keep the peace. Crowds tend to complicate their work. But *they will help you, both with advice and by keeping an eye on the event*. In return for police assistance, you have to avoid sowing the seeds for a possible fracas. Giving away things that have a strong appeal to teenagers is advertising for trouble. This is particularly true when the quantity is limited and put on a first come, first served basis.

The Dark at the Top of the Stairs

Operators who spend the entire day inside their restaurants have a tendency to forget that customers coming in from bright sunlight may be temporarily blinded in the subdued lighting of the interior. When the entryway includes steps, changes of floor level, chairs, guide ropes, or planters, a genuine danger to the customer exists. *The size of the lawsuit will depend on how seriously the customer has been injured on one of your obstacles.*

☑ *B/L Recommends:* If subdued lighting or darkness is part of your restaurant's ambience, *lead the customer into it in gradual stages.* Keep the entryway clear and reasonably well lighted. Diminish the lighting slightly in the lobby, and diminish it still further as the customers progress to their tables. This way the eyes can become accustomed to the change from outside sunlight.

EFFECTIVE

COST SAVINGS

Going into business gives you
the irrevocable right and privilege
to earn a profit
and the right and privilege
to go broke . . .
your own way.

5

EFFECTIVE COST SAVINGS

Everything you touch in business costs you money. Developing and pricing a menu correctly, or stopping the use of valuable cases of merchandise to hold open doors are both examples of effective cost savings.

The business is your responsibility. It is your money. You can waste it in many varied ways.

You can, through experience or study, apply yourself to practice and think economy in virtually everything that you do, without any loss of guest count, personnel, or profits.

You should not need a brown-out, black-out, or shortage of oil to make you a believer. Professionals always consider how they can effectively avoid the waste of time, people, and products to increase productivity and profits.

Restaurant Designers Should Pull K.P.

It would be a great thing for the industry and for humanity if restaurant designers had to work at least one week in each of their creations. The owner of a newly remodeled store called us the other day. Business was down, he said. He was considering making a heavy investment in advertising. We told him to hold off until we could get a look at the store. When we got there, we found that the place had been redesigned for "intimate dining." Translation: *The dining room was darker than the inside of a grill stone.* The partially exposed food prep area also had the lights turned down so as not to disturb the atmosphere. The nicest thing you could have done for the cook was to give him a flashlight. When the cook can't see, quality gets wiped off the menu. We told the owner he needed light fixtures more than advertising.

☑ *B/L Recommends:* Blindfolding cooks is a poor policy. *Check the wattage around the pass bar and in food preparation areas.* Grease smudges, dirt, and hair can become part of the entree when lighting is bad.

Boost Efficiency and Safety with Signage

Signage is the method of improving production by labeling, and by posting appropriate signs. Signage gets things stored in the proper place. *Signage simplifies the taking of inventory.* It improves traffic flow in the back end. New employees get oriented faster when signs tell them where things are. During rush hours, signage can eliminate confusion and save time.

☑ *B/L Recommends: Take a close look at employee work patterns.* In the reach-in, are the plastic and stainless steel containers marked on the outside to reflect contents? Or do cooks have to guess and grab when they are in a hurry? A small bottle of waterproof paint and a brush, available at hobby shops, can reduce the problem. One of the greatest accident hazards in the business comes about when deliveries are placed on stairs and passageways while somebody looks for the storeroom keys. "Keep Clear" signs in these areas will lessen the chances of employees being injured after stumbling over a carton or sack.

Salad Bar Tactics

When he added the salad bar to his operation, the client selected extra-small scoops for the salad dressings. He also arranged the salad bar more for eye appeal than economics. Some expensive ingredients were placed up front instead of at the back of the display. *Both decisions were costly.* When customers got to the salad dressings, they became triple dippers. This slowed the line during rush periods. Guests waiting to have their turn at the dressings used the time to embellish their salads with more ingredients. Naturally they picked the handy, expensive stuff up front.

☑ *B/L Recommends:* Moving the line is more important in a salad bar setup than using small scoops to try to conserve salad dressings. Another factor that adds to cost and waste is the *failure to chop vegetables into small, bite-size pieces.* Cucumber slices should be halved. Cauliflower pieces should be broken down. When guests at their tables attempt to cut raw vegetables on a heaped salad plate, things get messy and food is wasted.

How to Plan for Lower Printing Costs

Menu changes are rather traumatic events in the life of a restaurant. Even mere price alterations require some planning, retraining and additional supervision during the customer introduction phase. The actual reprinting of the menu is usually delegated to outside vendors. There are two ways to do it: costly or inexpensive. *Planning makes the difference.* Once you decide a menu price change is necessary, every day lost in the execution of the change costs money. You want to accomplish the changeover as rapidly as possible. Handing your printer a bunch of scribbled notes and an old menu is not the fastest most economical method to implement a menu changeover.

☑ *B/L Recommends:* The most frequent reason for reprinting a menu is to change prices. *When planning a printed menu, always provide for a quick, simple way to make price changes.* Do not allow the artist or production staff to print menu prices in more than one color. If you have to make a two color print price change, you add at least 30 percent to the cost and at least one day to the actual production time.

Take care of the original artwork for your menu. Wrap it and store in a dry, clean, cool area. Prolonging the life of the original art can save hundreds of dollars and considerable time when reprinting your menu. You can actually make minor price changes on the artwork yourself. Art stores supply something known as press-type. These are sheets of printed letters and numerals that can be cut or burnished right onto menu artwork. They come in hundreds of styles and sizes. The savings are at least ten to one over traditional methods of typesetting on small jobs. No time is lost waiting for printer proofs to okay. The fastest, most economical way to work is to supply the printer with "camera ready" art. This means your menu artwork requires no additional preparation. It is ready to be photographed, plated, and printed. Any extra steps outside this process require time and money.

These days, most printers do not inventory stocks of exotic papers, particularly the kinds used for menus. Printers order these heavy-duty papers from suppliers as required. *You can save two days or more in the printing time of your menu if you alert the printer to order paper in advance.* Or if you are going to bid out the reprint, be sure an exact sample of the paper is included with the bid specifications. When you select the printer for your job, have him or her order the paper immediately.

Each time you add a color to your menu, a day is added to the actual production time. If you require plastic lamination and your printer has to job out the process, this tacks another two days on to the delivery time. Die-cuts, special folds, tassels, embossing, metallic inks are all nice menu features, but each adds a day or more to the production schedule. *The time it takes for the production and delivery of your new menu is a hidden cost.* In determining how many frills you want on your printed menu, calculate the printer's cost plus those hidden charges, then make your decision.

Before sending the artwork for printing, have photo copies made. That way, staff training in the new price structure can move along while the menu is being printed.

Look Before You Book a Supplier

After many years in this business, one thing we know for certain: No deal with a supplier is forever. That's as it should be. The only real weapon a restaurateur has to protect him or herself in dealing with suppliers is threat of cancellation. *Things get sticky when the threat has to be turned into action.* In the process of quitting one supplier and bringing on another, managers frequently compound problems they are trying to resolve.

☑ **B/L Recommends:** If the time has arrived when your only option is to drop your current supplier, *think through how you are going to recruit a new one.* You know what you require from a supplier in the way of goods, deliveries, and billing. Now you want to match your list with the supplier most capable of meeting your needs. The best way to do it is to actually visit the premises of a potential new supplier. *Look over the facilities, trucks, and equipment.* How is the merchandise being handled? Are frozen products allowed to sit on the dock, or are they being properly held in a zero-degree box? What does the inventory look like? Is it a hand-to-mouth operation, or is there plenty of back-up stock on hand? Find out if the supplier bids on and gets government contracts. Government specs are strict and this is to your advantage. What system does the supplier have for keeping clients informed regarding seasonal price fluctuations and merchandise availability?

It takes time away from the job to check out suppliers in this fashion, but the investment will pay off in a more durable relationship with the supplier you eventually select.

Fishy Deals Don't Need Salt Water

It is well established that little fish get eaten by big fish. However, when a little fish develops a large set of jaws, it sometimes gets to be a big fish too. In the restaurant business, it is pretty well known that suppliers give better deals, rebates, allowances, and service to big accounts. *Little accounts get shafted.*

We have helped a couple of small accounts exercise their jaw muscles. In one case, an owner was told he had to come up with $125.00 to pay for the installation of soft drink dispensing equipment. We suggested he have another chat with the sales representative, based on some information we made available. The sales rep "managed" to take care of the installation costs. Wasn't that nice? In a more complex situation, we urged a client to swap specific cost information with comparable units outside his trading area. He did. Then he took on each of his sales representatives in a head-to-head meeting. He succeeded in arranging better ordering and delivery schedules and lower prices. He also won some cooperative advertising rebates for using and displaying certain products.

☑ **B/L Recommends:** *Become a tougher purchasing agent.* Do not accept prices, service, or maintenance charges at face value. Acquire as much outside pricing information as you can. Use it to hammer down prices from your own suppliers. You may never know whether you are getting the lowest prices or the best "special consideration." However, you know these things exist. Do not be timid in making sales reps aware of your knowledge. Sharp buyers get respect, better deals, and service.

What Will We Charge for the Hamburger?

On three separate occasions in one short span of time we encountered restaurant companies still using the old "3X" formula for menu pricing. That's the one that establishes the menu price of a dish at three times its cost.

In another case, we counseled an operator who was basing his menu prices on what the competition just down the street was charging. Both stores were getting no place rapidly, since his competition was operating on the same premise.

When the competition sets your menu prices, it also screws down the lid on your profits. The trouble with the 3X pricing formula is that it automatically establishes a 33% food cost. This probably worked well enough when labor was a dollar an hour and utilities were merely an incidental expense. But that was in the days when hamburger cost 35¢ a pound or less.

Inflation and spiraling costs for labor and utilities have almost forced menu pricing into the same class as fortune telling. *The confusion is costing a lot of companies heavy dollars on the bottom line.*

It is possible to get a firmer hold on profits with a pricing formula based on four absolutes. It takes some work on the front end, but it takes a lot of the gamble out of the menu pricing process. The four absolutes used in this method are: (1) the existing profit and loss statement; (2) the true (not approximate) meal cost; (3) the frequency of sale; (4) the desired level of profit.

☑ **B/L Recommends:** *Work on the principle that a dollar in the register must be used to pay all operating costs.* The existing P&L statement tells how much of each cash register dollar has to be spent in each area. For example:

P&L Operating Percentages		From the Register Dollar
Wages	30%	30¢
Employer taxes	3	3
Rent	10	10
Utilities	5	5
Maintenance	5	5
Insurance	3	3
Kitchen, janitorial	3	3
China, glass	2	2
Insurance, taxes	5	<u>5</u>
Total restaurant expenses less profit and food cost		66¢

The P&L in our abbreviated, hypothetical example shows that 66¢ of every dollar must be spent on all operating expenses before paying for food and taking a profit from the business.

Let's assume you wish a return of 10 percent on the bottom line before taxes. This is added to the payout in the same way as the P&L charges:

Profit	10%	<u>10¢</u>
Total restaurant expenses		
less food costs		76¢

The remainder is 24¢, or 24 percent, of the dollar in your register. *This is the food cost*. By calculating what percentage of each dollar must be spent for all expenses, and by including the profit we wish to make, we find out what the food cost must be to yield that profit. In this case, the food cost must be 24 percent. If the food cost were to be any higher than this, the difference would have to be made up from profits.

An accurate menu price cannot be determined until you know the total cost of each meal. Meal cost is the total expense of placing a properly portioned plate in front of the customer.

Let's price out a simple hamburger and fries, to illustrate the detail that goes into costing a meal, as opposed to estimating a cost:

	Cents
Hamburger patty (4 oz.) @ 80¢ lb.	20.0
Hamburger bun @ 72¢ doz.	6.0
French fries (3 oz. raw weight) @ 22¢ lb.	4.1
Fry shortening (amount used to fry 3 oz. fries)	
@ $17.00 per 50 lbs.	0.5
Lettuce garnish (½ oz.) @ $8.00 per 575 oz. case	0.7
Tomato slice (⅛th tomato) @ 10¢ ea.	1.7
Pickle chips (2 ea.) @ $1.95 per can of 650	0.6
Ketchup (est. ½ oz. customer portion) @ 28¢ per 14 oz.	1.0
Subtotal cost of food	34.6¢
Food wrap	0.8
Placemat	0.3
Napkin	0.3
Guest check	1.0
Total cost of food and paper	37.0

The same laborious process must be applied to every meal and every beverage on the menu. In today's market, it is no longer sufficient to simply say; ". . . a nickle for the bun, and 20¢ for the patty, and 5¢ for the garnish, and 5¢ for the fries." The costs of shortening are very real, *fry shortening is consumed when foods are fried*. Customers use ketchup, salt and pepper, and all other condiments with their meals. These things are food costs and must be figured into the total cost of the meal. If they are not, then profits will be lower than anticipated.

An important point to stress at this time is that there is no allowance in the figures for waste, theft, and overportioning. If these factors are not controlled, there is no way food costs can be determined with accuracy.

With our hypothetical hamburger, we have determined that the cost of placing the meal on the table is 37¢. We will use this figure later.

Guest check audits will tell how frequently any given item on the menu is sold. If an increase in prices is necessary to re-establish profitability, it stands to reason that increases in frequently sold foods will yield more sales volume than in foods that do not sell. If you sell 1,000 hamburgers a week, you can increase sales volume $100 by adding a dime to the menu price. On the other hand, if you sell one hot dog, the addition of a dollar to the menu price wouldn't really make any difference at all.

Small increases on the most popular items will return greater profits than large increases on things that do not sell. In fact, slight decreases in the price of unpopular items may create a market for them. If nothing else, it will cause a better and more rapid turnover of stock.

The most unproductive step is to increase the price of everything on the menu. This is immediately obvious to the steady customers and creates a "buy down" situation. A buy down means that you will serve just as many people, but have less to show for it.

After all these preliminaries, it should finally be possible to establish a menu price for our hamburger.

In the P&L calculations, we determined you must hold food costs at 24 percent if you are to attain a 10 percent profit. The question is: What menu price must be used to sell a 37¢ hamburger at a 24 percent food cost? First divide 100 percent by 24 percent to get a multiplication factor:

$$100 \div 24 = 4.17$$

Each meal cost must be multiplied by 4.17 to determine the menu price. In the instance of our hamburger:

$$37¢ \times 4.17 = \$1.54$$

The menu price is $1.54, or if rounded off to the nearest nickle, $1.55. Every hamburger sold at $1.55 will have a food cost of 24 percent and there will be a 10 percent profit resulting from the sale.

The final point to make in structuring menu prices is that eating is an emotional experience. Paying the check is also an emotional experience. Some foods are priced as high as the public will accept. On these there is a psychological barrier that the public will not pass. Among these barrier foods are:

a glass of milk or cola; a bowl of soup; a cup of coffee or tea, and a piece of pie.

Every operator must evaluate his or her own community and adjust those prices that have bumped against the psychological barrier. For a sound menu pricing formula, you must add two additional ingredients: common sense and good business judgment.

Inflation Strikes Down Cost Controls

One of the pernicious effects of inflation is that *restaurant executives are becoming numb to escalating costs*. This syndrome is dangerous. It erodes the effectiveness of good cost control. When inflation is accepted as the reason for increased expenses, its logical to assume: Inflation has to be hurting competition, suppliers, and customers alike, and therefore, the best answer is to increase menu prices.

Simple isn't it? Once inflation is assumed as the reason for increased costs, management closes the door to all other options except raising prices. *Good cost control is no longer an imperative*.

What happens, and is happening more and more, can be illustrated by a recent experience. We were in the back end of an outlet belonging to a long-established full service chain. We watched a cook/trainee pour a sack of dry mix into a Hobart bowl. About four pounds fell on the floor. The trainee did not put the collar on the bowl. The store manager saw the blunder: "Watch it, man! That stuff costs 14 cents a pound. You're wastin' it." End of message. The manager did not attempt to show the trainee the right way to fill the bowl. Obviously he did not feel it was that important.

Ten years earlier, the manager's actions would have earned him a blast that would have made the Richter scale. Ten years ago, the chain was producing a higher profit percentage on volume than it is today. Between that time and now there have been 16 across-the-board menu price increases. Management emphasis has drifted from tight cost controls to an attitude of "it isn't worth the trouble. We'll make it up on the next price hike." When any form of waste is tolerated through the expedient of price hikes, only one thing can happen. The waste problem is going to grow faster than profits.

☑ *B/L Recommends:* Maintain a constant war on waste. Do not get confused as to the identity of the true enemy. *Inflation doesn't help you. Waste can kill you*. The manager cited above was promoted and put in control of a store with an annual volume of over one million dollars. Incredible as it sounds, nobody on the company's sophisticated executive staff bothered to explain the facts of good cost control:

A) Supplies are delivered to the back door at one price.

B) Once inside the door, all food items assume menu value price;

C) A smashed egg does not represent a six cent loss. That egg sells for 40 cents, or whatever the menu says.

The logic is based on the fact the clumsy cook that dropped the egg is on a salary. The uniform he or she wears has to be paid for, as does all the rest of the food and equipment in the store including the cleanser and towel to wipe up the mess. A manager that does not get this point over to employees is going to run excessively high food costs.

The manager's training also neglected to stress the value of practical example when issuing instructions to employees. He felt it wasn't necessary for him to install the bowl collar and lift a heavy sack just to show how a 56 cent error can be corrected. When he was told the mistake created a busted formula with a sales value of $148.00, he changed his thinking. Good cost controls start with good training in waste prevention.

Dish Replacements Cost More Than List Price

There is a huge chart on the wall in the food preparation area of one of the country's largest hotels. Broken cups and plates, mangled knives, forks and spoons are anchored to the board. Beside each item is a price supposedly indicating the replacement cost. What the chart really explains best is why the hotel company is having a hard time making its foodservice operation produce a profit. The prices are taken right from an outdated catalog. Even if the chart had reflected current catalog prices, it would accurately depict only part of the true replacement costs. There are about a half dozen hidden charges tacked on to the catalog pricetag.

First, any breakage limits the restaurant's ability to produce revenue until a replacement is actually in place. Very few stores operate on a running inventory. Tableware gets replaced when it is apparent there is a shortage. That is, when there are no cups to put coffee in, and when there are no platters for the steaks. It always happens during rush periods, so the floor is slowed down and this means sales are lost.

People have to be paid to receive, stock and issue replacement items. The first pass through the dishwasher is another expense. The purchase money tied up in dishes sitting on a storeroom shelf could be earning bank interest rates. But you have to have backup supplies because few employees believe that gravity really works. Of course, the storage space for the material has to be paid for, along with the appropriate taxes. While a cup may be catalog priced at 70¢, its actual cost can well be over a dollar or more.

☑ *B/L Recommends:* At the next employee meeting, conduct a quiz. Hold up a half dozen different items of tableware. Have employees write down what they think the costs are for replacing each item. Just before the end of the meeting, announce who was the most nearly correct. At the same time, explain the points outlined above. *You will see a marked improvement in tableware replacement costs.*

Putting the Brakes on Breakage

At the annual manager's meeting, they said some good things about Harry J. His store had the lowest dish replacement record for the year. His record was so good that his fellow managers suspected Harry was using rubber plates. What happened was that Harry realized he alone could not hold down breakage. *He delegated the job to the floor hostesses*. Every month he met with the hostesses and reviewed progress on this one point. *By locating the points where most breakage occurred*, they devised better dish handling techniques. Month-to-month breakage percentages were diagrammed on the employee bulletin board. Everyone in the house was breakage conscious.

☑ *B/L Recommends:* A lot of problems exist in stores because nobody wants to commit the time and energy to clearing them up. Breakage costs can be cut. But it takes more than just an occasional admonishment from the manager. It requires an ongoing program, with appropriate delegation of duties and periodic progress checks.

"Your Cups Runneth Over"

Usually this is a blessing, but in the fast food business where paper and plastic goods are used so extensively this saying should read: "Your cost-of-cups runneth over." Count the tremendous number of cups that individual employees use and throw away several times each shift. People drink water, milk, soft drinks, shakes, juices, and other items throughout their shifts and use a new cup or glass each time. We cost-checked one chain and found the average employee was using five cups per shift. Five cups per person multiplied by several hundreds of employees each day added up to thousands of lost dollars per year. The nine-year-old chain admitted this practice had been going on since its inception. Not anymore it isn't!

☑ *B/L Recommends:* Purchase for each employee his or her own private mug or plastic glass to be used at all times when consuming liquids of any type. Make sure each mug or glass has the employee's name on it and that there is a hook or shelf to keep all such drinking containers on when not in use. The savings will be astounding, and the effort will produce the excellent side effect of making employees realize you are serious about cost controls.

Don't Get Soaked for Towel Laundry

Indiscriminate use of towels gets expensive. Putting them under a lock and key is not too practical from an efficiency standpoint. A better way to keep towel laundry expenses in line is to establish a system for towel use, and make sure the crew abides by it.

☑ *B/L Recommends: Every towel should be used for no less than three days*. The first day, fresh, clean towels go in the front and are used to wipe down tables in view of the customers. The second day they are used in the kitchen. The third day, in the dishwashing area. Each night, towels that have

already been used for three days are put in permanent containers with a little
bleach and soap. In the morning, they are rinsed in the dish machine on the
rinse cycle.

Holding the Line on Energy Costs

Some pundits maintain the energy crunch is going to ease a little for the
short term. Others say the long term prospects are gloomy indeed. No matter,
everyone is convinced that utility bills are going to keep going up. It is more
important than ever to take care of small maintenance problems around the
store *immediately*. Frost-coated freezers and refrigerators are a profit drain. A
faucet that leaks only one drop of water a second will waste 400 gallons in a
year.

☑ *B/L Recommends: Start an energy conservation file.* There is a lot of
material appearing in trade journals and being released by government
agencies that can save you money and help the country conserve energy. Clip
the material that is applicable to your operation and *use it as the basis for a
comprehensive energy saving effort.*

Check what tools and supplies you have in the house to handle minor repair
jobs, such as the replacement of faucet washers and gaskets. Put everything
into a kit. List the contents and the jobs that can be taken care of on the
outside of the box. Also include an illustrated how-to-fix-it book.

When a Cover-Up Is Necessary

One client uses a large steam table for his dish-ups. The popularity of some
of his specials was way off and business itself was not too good. He was
considering a drastic and costly menu overhaul along with price changes. The
plan might have worked, but it wasn't necessary. What *was* necessary was
some staff schooling. *Food servers were not using covers on the hotel pans.*
They thought it was too much bother. Naturally, a lot of the products seemed
to have made a stopover in the arctic on the way to the table.

Food servers today are just not getting good basic training. We explained to
the staff that a steam table supplies more than enough heat on the bottom of
the pan, but that all the heat does not get through the food to the topmost
level. What does, is quickly dissipated into the air.

At best, this means that the guest receives an unevenly heated entree.
However some of the food may be falling below the magic 160 degree mark
and be subject to bacterial growth. Finally, an uncovered pan offers no
protection from foreign objects. Covers, we explained, are a vital part of steam
table quality control. As soon as food servers started using the cover-up
program, there was less variation in the quality of the entrees being sold, and
business started returning to normal.

☑ *B/L Recommends:* Little things like uncovered pans can and do hurt the
business, because the product is hurt. Many times employees are totally

unaware of the implications of their actions. *Covered hotel pans in the steam table maintain heat with a lower utility cost;* covers protect food from contamination; they help retain the moisture originally in the food. *Don't keep these trade secrets from your employees.*

Disposing of Disposer Difficulties

Why is it that workers insist on treating the garbage disposer unit as though it's a piece of garbage? This tremendously valuable tool gets a daily beating like no other piece of equipment in the store. When a disposer coughs and quits, the guy who has been feeding it coasters, napkins, and placemats acts outraged. *On a diet like that, who wouldn't quit?* Workers are invariably told not to let frilled toothpicks and paper goods get into the disposer. Sooner or later a couple of pieces accidently slip through and the machine manages to digest the stuff. The worker sees this and a bad habit comes to life.

☑ *B/L Recommends:* Good discipline is needed to keep a disposer in action. When a disposer goes down, so does kitchen efficiency. Most of the time the reason is human error. Frequent stoppages may indicate something needs fixing, but not in the machine—*in the operator's head.* One thing that creates disposer jams is turning the power off as soon as the noise level drops. When the machine noise goes from a roar to a hum, it indicates the scraps have cleared the machine. They have. *They are now in the drain immediately below the disposer.* They solidify there and start clogging the pipe. To prevent this, the disposer should be run with a full water flow for at least one minute after the noise level drops. The action flushes the scraps into the street sewer.

When Do-It-Yourself Means Doing It Wrong

Booth and table damages can cause problems beyond a costly invoice for repairs. Managers attempt to delay that inevitable call to the repair service by doing their own jury-rigged work. These "temporary" patch jobs are about as popular with customers as fricasseed barbed wire. Instead of tip revenue, *the waiter or waitress on station starts receiving a lot of verbal flak from unhappy customers.* He or she, of course, becomes unhappy. When an unhappy serving person serves an unhappily seated customer, it's bad news for business, too. Poor repairs are what earns a store the appellation of "crappy place."

☑ *B/L Recommends: Don't kid yourself with do-it-yourself repair work.* A junky booth or table automatically makes guests wary of what is offered on the menu. If competent repairs cannot be made immediately, it is sometimes better to shut down a booth until things can be properly fixed. When this happens, floor stations should be rearranged to help compensate the waiter or waitress for reduced tip revenue. This should not happen too often if serving personnel are told to immediately report minor booth damages.

Equipment Suppliers Don't Need Your Money

One reason the equipment supply business is so profitable is that restaurant owners and managers buy more gear than they should. *Big bucks are thrown away on repair, replacement, and financing charges.* Many charges could be postponed, some even eliminated, by effective preventive maintenance ("PM").

☑ *B/L Recommends:* Get your preventive maintenance program out in the open. If PM instructions are confined to a store manual, or worse, only shown in the manufacturer's manual, equipment is not going to get the attention required. *Another way to louse up a PM effort is to verbally assign tasks that need to be done on a weekly and monthly basis.* People forget things. Every PM requirement in the house should appear on checklists. The lists can be arranged for weekly, monthly, quarterly, even semi-annual PM. All instructions for handling each PM chore, with diagrams if available, should appear on the checklists. *It is always better to use up paper than risk a possible employee injury,* or damage to expensive equipment.

Once the lists are put together by week and month, organize the task allocation: things to be done by the cook, the service assistant and so on. At the top of each checklist place a line for name and date. At the end of each list place a signature line. Then photocopy the whole works. You need enough copies of each list to last one year. When this is done, write the date the list is to be used on each checklist. Place all the checklists in date sequence with the current date on top of the pile.

Now you are ready to assign PM work. Put the name of the person assigned to do the checklist work next to the dateline. Have him or her sign on the bottom line when all tasks are completed. Be sure all items are checked off, then file the list. You will find *PM work is accomplished more diligently when employees certify their work by their own signatures.* It takes a little time up front organizing this system, but it saves many, many hours of repeatedly assigning tasks verbally and then closely supervising completion. You will get better PM work, fewer things will be overlooked, and you'll have lower costs and a more efficient operation.

Practice Dishwashing Economy

Have you talked to your dishwasher lately? He or she operates a mighty expensive piece of machinery. A conveyor dish machine, or any dish machine, wastes energy unless operated at capacity. To run a conveyor only partly loaded consumes just as much electricity, gas to heat the water, water, and soap as a full load.

☑ *B/L Recommends:* During non-peak periods, *turn off the dish machine*. Assign other duties to the operator. Save the dishes, glasses, and flatware until enough have been accumulated to make a capacity load.

Open Sesame

Sometimes doors just open up all by themselves. No one is responsible. No one will admit to leaving critical doors open. Walk-in refrigerators and freezer doors separate warm air from air chilled to specified temperatures. Any great loss of cold will cause losses of food and food quality.

☑ *B/L Recommends:* Install a simple alternating light, with a switch, and contact plate (as one of our chains did) above the door and jamb of all walk-in boxes. Whenever doors are opened, the light bulb fixed above the doors on the wall will blink on and off continuously until the door has once more been *completely* closed. Should the doors be left open an inch or a mile, on purpose or by accident, the blinking light will remind all that valuable cold air is escaping. This danger signal once installed for a small cost will save great actual and potential losses.

For Economy, Use Those Rubber Spats

They cost pennies and save dollars, yet rubber spatulas are about the most elusive piece of equipment in a galley. They get broken, thrown away and only infrequently reordered. In working with clients, we show them the cost of operating without rubber spats by simply checking the contents of the dumpster outside the back door. Invariably $2.00 or more in wasted food clings to the sides and bottoms of cans and containers.

☑ *B/L Recommends:* *Reread the above paragraph.*

SALES
PROMOTION

Consider the mosquito as an example.
He rarely gets a slap on the back
until he gets to work.

6

SALES PROMOTION

We all "sell" something; a product, meal, service, or an idea. Selling need not always be associated with high-pressure tactics or glib hucksters. Selling, similarly, doesn't have to display an obvious price tag. Few of us want to appear greedy or selfish as we strive to earn the almighty buck.

We, as salespeople, know that we must deliver a benefit to our end-users. It is our business to give guests an eating experience. Take, for example, the term "suggestive selling" that we so often try to pound into our service personnel in order to sell more side items and desserts to increase sales and profits. The intent of suggestive selling always seems to have a price tag attached to it. But we'd like to suggest that suggestive selling is asking guests whether they want cream and sugar with their coffee, some condiments, or another napkin. Helping a guest to better enjoy a meal is suggestive selling.

Foodservice and hospitality people daily deliver many free, wonderful services and accommodations to guests, but often do so without a purpose or plan.

Management should use every possible sales promotional idea to get guests excited about better values and enjoyment and, at the same time, motivate employees to become involved in the delivery of superior eating experiences to their guests.

How's Your P.R. These Days?

Have you ever considered that publicity and public relations can and should be an integral part of your business, no matter how large or small your operation? It can be the next best thing to word-of-mouth advertising. Favorable publicity stories can tell people something new, exciting, and interesting about you, your store, your employees, customers, and whatever it is that may be going on in your business. Haven't you wondered why certain names always seem to pop up in the restaurant columns? They do not get there by accident!

☑ **B/L Recommends:** Develop a list of each newspaper, radio and television station that covers your marketing area. Add to it the names and addresses of all editors of the trade papers and magazines in our industry. Get in the habit of sending to all media interesting pieces of information and unusual happenings. Use a simple letterhead. Mark it: "PRESS RELEASE," or "FOR IMMEDIATE RELEASE." Write out all the facts: who, why, when, where, and how. Do not try to be too clever. Just state the facts. You read the trade papers, copy the style used there. Include a short story about your company for background information. Supply glossy black and white photographs if possible.

Maintain a scrap book of all releases you send out, whether they are published or not. Local and trade media are happy to receive good P.R. copy. They will use it if you are smart enough to send it. Do not forget restaurant, real estate business, fashion, and society editors. Each can use good timely copy too.

What's Your Angle? Can You Promote It?

Call it a concept or a gimmick, but all of us have an angle for which we hope we will be remembered and patronized. Food-oriented people develop signature specialties. Creative people add decorative gimmicks to attract customers. Many of us have laughed all the way to the bank with the simplest of ideas, while others have almost knocked themselves out with menus and complicated systems, which left them with little or no time to properly plan promotions to take advantage of their uniqueness.

☑ **B/L Recommends:** One well-established dinnerhouse we know that features excellent Spanish food recently made a very simple, unique, and straightforward offer to local high school and college students who have successfully passed their Spanish finals. He offers a special price-off discount. This promotion is simple, direct, and importantly, in keeping with his concept. Each quarter or semester he sends announcements of his offer to Spanish instructors asking that they post his offer for their students to read. Many teachers have brought groups of students to the restaurants to take advantage of the dinner discounts. This word-of-mouth campaign rings true. It is high class even though it is a discount deal. Spanish students are encouraged to speak the language, read the bilingual menu, and order in Spanish as they learn to enjoy real Spanish food.

Future customers? *Sí*. A newsworthy event? *Sí*. Will local scribes pick up on this promotion? *Sí*.

Wishing Does Not Make It So

"Boy, I wish I had thought of that." That is what many managers tell themselves after reading a favorable newspaper item about what a competing outfit is doing.

It is quite possible to make wishes like this come true. The services of a high-powered P.R. expert are not needed to do it.

☑ *B/L Recommends:* Study the elements of the competitor's story closely. What made it unique enough to appear in print? Once you isolate the unusual facets of the story, you know what the editors like, or are willing to accept. Now, *what you have to do is put a new twist on the item by whatever means you have at your disposal.*

Use a lined pad. Divide the page into two columns. On one side write down the unique elements of the original story. In the other column you list everything you can do to come up with a comparable news item. You do not want to duplicate the original, you want to produce a better, more interesting product. Once you have your combination put together, play it back to the local editor and find out what he or she thinks. You do not have to always follow someone's local lead. Study out-of-town restaurant pages. Pick up on the stuff that has not appeared in your own newspaper.

Beat the Drums, Santa Claus Is Coming to Town

If your banquet room or party area is not fully booked for the holiday time by mid-November, get busy. Aside from the profits parties generate at the end of the year, *they introduce a whole lot of new people to your food and service.* It is the best possible type of advertising you can do for your business. Attracting customers in December helps overcome the traditional February/March business slump. This is so important that if you are not going to have time to devote to promoting party business during this period, hire someone to do it. Or assign one of your top-flight employees to work on the project part of each day. Award a bonus when the project is completed.

☑ *B/L Recommends:* The first thing to do is to put together a business mailing and contact list. Start with the people that booked parties last year. Next, acquire the membership list of your local Chamber of Commerce. Also, use the yellow pages and newspaper classified section. Check the help-wanted section to obtain the names of good-sized companies in your market area. *Get the names of the people charged with making party and banquet arrangements for their firms.* If you can't get a name, address communications to: "Director of Employee Relations."

The message you want to project is that you are ready to professionally assist neighboring companies in creating truly festive holiday observances. Contact instant print shops in your area. Some offer pre-printed cards. These self-mailers can be tailored to your requirements very economically. There are a lot of holiday themes to choose from. Work out a system of mailings combined with follow-up phone calls. When the promotion is over, carefully seal and label the contact list and file it for later use.

Profiting on Good News

When the feeder airline announced it was moving its headquarters to a new city, the news brought cheer to the designated city's restaurant owners. It brought one of them, the operator of a small chain, several hundred thousand dollars in profits. He did not just pass along the good news—he did something about it. *He put in a long distance call to the operations chief of the airline and invited the whole company to his stores for dinner* when they arrived in town. He had dinner invitations printed, one for each of the 300 families making the move. He mailed the invitations to the airline's old headquarters. The company distributed the guest invitations along with its transfer instructions. Since that time, the airline has acquired two other lines. Each time, the new people arriving in town received their invitations. The chain has had no problem with volume slippage for a long time. The owner doesn't have any problems with airline reservations either.

☑ *B/L Recommends:* Get in the habit of analyzing how events happening near your restaurant *can be translated into potential profits*. With a little practice, it becomes almost automatic. You will know you have the hang of doing it right when your competitors start calling you "Lucky."

Coupons Can Be Clip Jobs

Mistakes come in all sizes. Fry station miscues only offend a customer or two. Restaurant advertising goof-ups can aggravate hundreds of people. *Announcing to 245,000 newspaper readers you don't know what day it is, qualifies as a big blunder.* A nationally known restaurant chain did just this in a major city. Caught up in the coupon craze, this outfit advertised a chicken dinner special. The coupon expired July 31. It appeared in the paper August 8. They will have to sell 2,071 more hamburgers to recoup the cost of the ad, which is no big deal. What is going to be harder to recover is the prestige and public confidence in which this chain has invested millions of advertising dollars.

☑ *B/L Recommends:* Coupons can be hazardous to a restaurant's health. If you are using coupons in newspaper advertising, *get a proof of the ad in advance of publication*. Or if the deadline is close, *have the ad text read over the telephone by someone in the newspaper advertising department*.

There are more problems with coupons than wrong expiration dates. For one thing, returned coupons are seldom analyzed correctly. Processing instructions are spotty. This embarrasses serving personnel and guests. Further, if the offer is really valuable, it can give your cash handlers a nifty pay raise, one you know nothing about.

This Giveaway Got Away

The drink 'n' steak dinner combination offer looked good on paper. When the promotion was put on the tabletalkers, the customers loved it. Two weeks later, *management found out they had a monster on their hands*. The way the promotion was organized, to get one drink in front of a guest bartenders were pouring two, sometimes three gratis highballs. Waiters were told to use a code word when ordering the promotional drink from the bar. The idea was to avoid running the promotional tickets through the bar's cash register, which would cause confusion when the check was settled at the front cashstand. What this actually did was parcel out the responsibility for beverage control between bartenders and waiters. It created the type of climate wherein booze evaporates in quantity and very seldom leaves a trace.

☑ *B/L Recommends:* Once the mechanics of a promotion are set down on paper, *it is necessary to study all the interface points involved in the action*. An interface is where the responsibility for an action passes from one individual to another. It begins with what management says to the staff about the promotion. It includes what management says to suppliers regarding backup; what the serving person says to customers; what the serving person says to cooks and bartenders; what the cashier says to the departing guest. All these points will have some sort of effect on the ultimate success or failure of the promotion. If a promotion looks good on paper but fizzles on execution, take a hard look at the interface points first.

Intrigue 'Em with Initials

Plotting new ways across the serving person/customer communications gap also opens new avenues of profit. Better suggestive selling is possible when customer curiosity is piqued, and then gratified by a friendly exchange with the waiter or waitress.

☑ *B/L Recommends:* Imprint some badges or ribbons with the initials T.O.H.W.? Then your people will be able to say with a smile, "Try Our House Wine?" An explanation and a sales message, all in one handy package. You can do it with soups, sandwiches, whatever. Just don't leave the promotion on the floor too long. The novelty wears out along with the ribbons.

An Oenological Tip

Table tents are great for boosting wine sales. There is also a simple way to make them doubly effective with very little expense or bother.

☑ *B/L Recommends:* Add wine glasses to table setups after 4:00 p.m. This quietly suggests that discerning diners always enjoy wine with their meals. Even if the waiter or waitress forgets to suggest wine, the empty glass is on the table as a gentle reminder to the guest.

The Hat Trick

Purists may argue the origin of this sports term. Originally, the term "hat trick" referred to the cricket player who pitched three bowls and took out three opposing players in succession. A local haberdasher used to award a new hat to the player who performed this difficult feat. Today, we use the term to mean that a hockey player has scored three goals in any one game. We are not sure any businesses have ventured forth to award any free hats. However, we do know of a successful sports promotion that carries a great deal of word-of-mouth advertising

☑ *B/L Recommends:* If your store can handle a *big rush*, do the following: run an ad or two in your local school or university newspaper. State that you will give a free soft drink, free fries, free coffee, or some house specialty (with or without a purchase) to every student who shows a student I.D. card and patronizes your establishment immediately following the game whenever their school team scores (x) number of points or more. You select the team. And, you select the magic number, i.e. one hundred points in basketball, thirty-five points in football, five goals in hockey, etc. Check past records to get a fair idea of the possible frequency wherein you may have to pay off on your bet. Your name will be the talk of the game as students will literally scream when the score gets close to your promise "as advertised." They will applaud and yell the name of your store as they plan to meet at your place immediately following the game. You become the hero win or lose. This is a great way to earn a reputation. Your competitors will wish they had made a similar offer. We tip our hat to you for pulling off this trick.

Profitwise, Dessert Sales Are Not Too Fattening

There comes a time in the life of every young manager when he or she figures out that *dessert sales can fatten the profit picture*. Generally, he or she calls a meeting to inform the staff of the discovery and to exhort them to greater dessert sales. Since the pros have all heard the routine before, this cannot be expected to measurably improve dessert sales. On the other hand, the meeting will not be a total waste of time. Some of the veterans will stop giving out ice cream and pie when their friends order coffee. They now know the boss is watching the goodies. If the manager is really tenacious, the next thing he or she will likely try is a contest to increase dessert sales. Since only waiters or waitresses can compete, this can be depended on to irk the rest of the crew. That's not the big problem. When the prize is really attractive, and there are posters in the locker room and daily messages and hoopla promoting the event, *there is a serious danger the contest will be a success*. If that happens, volume will probably drop faster than a bus tray with greasy handgrips.

☑ *B/L Recommends:* Handle incentive competitions with caution. *Stay away from dessert sale competitions in particular.* If the pros really decide to sell desserts, they will begin telling customers about the terrible thing going on in the store. Waitresses *must* sell desserts. So if the customer does not order a dessert, she, the waitress, will probably lose her job. Her kids will go hungry and they will all have to sleep in the street. In order to protect the waitress from the nasty company, the customer feels he or she has to buy a dessert. It's a grand tactic for winning contests. The only trouble is that it knocks off customers almost as efficiently as botulism. *Customer coercion only works once*. Additionally, there is the questionable wisdom of tying up a booth for an extra 15 minutes during the rush while a 75 cent dessert is being consumed. That can cost some table turns and give the house a reputation for being slow. From a business standpoint, desserts look mighty attractive. Just keep in mind that they come loaded with more than just calories.

Take a Good Look at Take-Out Business

We'd like to tip our bain-marie to Maxim's of Paris. They are doing exactly what we have recommended to several clients recently—promoting take-out business. When it's done right, it's smart and profitable. Maxim's is doing just that. While most full service establishments still regard take-outs as a pain in the galley, there are advanced thinkers in the industry starting to take advantage of the take-out potential.

In recent years, millions of dollars have been poured into merchandising take-out meals. *A huge market has been created*. Container technology has gone ahead at the same pace. Despite the advances, the general public's menu selection is still confined mainly to chop suey, fried chicken or fish 'n chips. From a business standpoint, it makes as much sense as a three-record jukebox.

Another aspect to consider is that restaurant galleys are far from cost-efficient operations. All that expensive equipment only performs at capacity a few short hours every day. The payments, taxes, and rent go on around the clock.

Take-out orders don't tie up tabletops. In effect, increasing take-out business is like adding an extension to the dining room for the cost of some paper goods.

☑ *B/L Recommends:* Take a new look at what can be done through take-out merchandising. *Consider establishing a take-out menu*, one that features dishups, stews, casseroles, baked BBQ ribs, items that can be prepped during slow periods in the back end. Give the take-out menu to regular customers and use it as a mailer to homes and businesses in your market area. Be sure and call attention to special rates for large parties. Create a system of procedure for processing take-out orders that does not conflict with rush hour galley operations. You can even establish an off-premises outlet for take-out. Maxim's is doing this in a co-op arrangement.

A word of advice: If you embark on a take-out promotion, structure take-out activity as a subsidiary to your regular operation. In other words, arrange things so the take-out side buys product from the restaurant operation. Cost control is better, and the system can subsequently develop into a profitable spin-off when the time is right.

Monday Night Football & Baseball

Sports fans are in a class by themselves. Given the opportunity, men by the score (and women too) will station themselves by their television sets for hours on end to watch their favorite teams and sporting events. Restaurant operators have for years felt the impact of athletics on weekends, at World Series time, on Super Bowl days, and now on several evenings during the week. Most bars and many restaurants tune in their own TV sets to the events to satisfy their guests. Some give away popcorn, peanuts, and team caps to get everyone into the spirit. Meanwhile, at home, meals are interrupted by whatever may be on television. Family members are upset, ignored, and left out of the fun.

☑ *B/L Recommends:* Increase your weekday and evening business. Offer special promotions, catering, and take-out packs to those sports fans who want to stay at home to watch TV. Encourage families to "picnic" right in their own homes. Make the family pack and price attractive. Offer a no-muss, no-fuss meal for couples and families. It is a better than even bet that they will take you up on your promotion.

Everyone Loves a Free Sample

Haven't you felt especially warm toward delicatessens, bakeries, and other specialty stores that offer a taste of their more exotic items to customers before they buy? Aren't you glad to go back to those stores?

☑ *B/L Recommends:* One independent owner we know regularly practices a promotion that is designed to show he cares about his guests, while he introduces menu items to them. On slow evenings, and when the mood strikes him, he will slice foods into hors d'oeuvre-size tidbits. He uses toothpicks or tongs to serve his guests a free taste. He tries to do it personally, to both chat with and sell his ideas to his guests. His waitresses and waiters eagerly follow his example. Tips are better. People are happier. New foods are introduced to more customers in a genuine, believable person-to-person manner.

Building a Sunday Brunch

Sunday Brunch is a growing, highly popular weekly event for families almost everywhere. That's not to say that a brunch promotion will work for all restaurant operations. We have talked to operators who have tried brunches and been disappointed with the results. They complain mainly about the slow growth of the promotion, and the high advertising costs. After reviewing some unproductive brunch promotions, we have to conclude the *lack of public interest results when operators try to develop the action along conventional promotion lines*. Popping a couple of bottles of champagne and a couple of ads on newspaper restaurant pages does not guarantee success.

☑ *B/L Recommends:* Brunch promotions have to be handled with skill and care. *A Sunday Brunch cannot be developed as an extension of the regular weekday breakfast rush*, no matter how many frills are added. The ambience of Sundays has to be relaxed, cordial and gracious. The guests are taking part in an event, not just a meal. Attention has to be directed toward heightening this effect. This should cover everything from the greeting at the door, the music, the seating, and the food presentation, to the farewell. Once these factors are in place, the easiest basic audience to attract is the store's regular Monday-Friday trade. That does not take a big ad outlay. Printed miniature Sunday Brunch menus can be handed to guests during the week. The service staff, given the right words to say, can promote the event to guests by inviting them to become part of the Sunday event. Please the regulars with a good Sunday Brunch and their word-of-mouth advertising will put this promotion over the top.

When Banquets Bomb, Think About Buffets

Banquet business is not what it used to be. Those folks stuck with large, moribund rooms know what we mean. Spiraling costs for labor, maintenance, taxes, and promotion have pushed banquet prices to the point of no profitable return. Associations and other groups are cutting back on engagements. Many say they have problems getting members to attend the fewer affairs that are scheduled. *However, the trend is not irreversible.*

We work with one restaurant/banquet room operator who has done a magnificent job in putting his room back on the profit side of the ledger. A top line professional, this man decided to offer, one night a week, a very special dinner to discerning guests. He deliberately planned his events to run a high food cost. Then he worked out the service pattern to provide a low labor expense. One night it's seafood—all kinds, nothing but the best in heaping servings. The following week it's barbecue night, with big steaming slabs of beef and pork in a tangy sauce. Then, South of the Border night and so on. Customers serve themselves with whatever they wish from the vegetable and salad offerings at the head of the line. Kitchen help carve and serve the meat items. Two waitresses serve beverages and desserts, one or two service assistants clear tables. The room spins like a top. An average night in the formerly empty room grosses about $3,200, with a 50 percent food cost and 15 percent labor.

☑ *B/L Recommends:* A good food value gets customers like nothing else. But this means a high food cost and it has to be offset by a low labor factor. Direct mail was used to launch this promotion. The owner used his own mailing list and another that he borrowed from a nearby golf club. *Word of mouth is now the mainstay of the promotion.* He still backs the effort with a small newspaper ad weekly. When guests leave the room, they receive an announcement of the dinner program for the weeks ahead. *This owner has also started booking buffet nights for some large organizations.* It is an interesting new way to merchandise a banquet room. The method avoids the crassness of "all you can eat," yet convinces guests that they received top value for their restaurant dollar.

"Specials" Need Special Handling

"Specials of the Day" can produce outstanding profits with the right type of in-house merchandising. Too often, the merchandising aspect is given only passing attention. This reduces "special" sales during the rush. It also tends to hang up production in the kitchen, as cooks try to cope with a wide variety of food orders.

We know one manager who is losing a few hundred dollars a week simply because he persists in using abbreviations on the blackboard that advertises his luncheon specials. *He attempts to talk to customers in the same shorthand that employees use to process food orders.* Most of the customers are not aware that if they order a "Hot CB San," they will be served a Hot Corned Beef Sandwich. The specially priced "HFS" is a loser, as well. As a Hot Fudge Sundae, it would probably do very well.

☑ *B/L Recommends: Specials of the day have to be prominently merchandised inside the store.* We like blackboard type of displays because the format suggests that what is offered is new and fresh. Menu clip-ons, on the other hand, appear to be an added thought, like a postscript to a letter. An adjective or two in your message to customers never hurts. But spell everything out. *Use clear words and prices.* Never assume guests understand restaurant shorthand.

Coupons Can Be a Curse

Through newspaper coupon promotions, *a lot of restaurants are busy printing their own money.* Coupon advertisements returned to the restaurant are often handled just like cash. Coupon values can range as high as five dollars or more, as in the case of a two-for-one dinner special. When this happens, more than just potential customers get attracted by the offer. There is a five-unit fast food chain that has been regularly using coupons as their main advertising thrust for the past two years. One store consistently produces as many coupons as the other four units combined. The store is a marginal operation and management is concerned that discontinuing coupons will sink the eatery even further in the red. "Folks in that neighborhood just love coupons," is management's contention. They are kidding themselves. The fact is the chain has lousy guest check audit practices, and the night manager at the big coupon-producing outlet knows it. The company is not only being ripped off, they have been investing in an advertising program for the last two years that has been a waste of money.

☑ *B/L Recommends:* Before embarking on a coupon promotion, make certain all audit controls are in effect and working. *You should require redeemed coupons to be stapled to the guest check,* not just dumped under the register cash tray. If guest checks do not carry serial numbers, get some that do before breaking a coupon promotion. Where possible, use a special cash register key mark to indicate coupon redemption on the tape. Secure or

:

cancel redeemed coupons on a daily basis to avoid recycling.

Crazy Days

"Okay, troops," said the manager, "Costume Day this month will be the twenty-third. What's it gonna be this time? Remember we want everyone to have fun and act a little crazy, but give our guests top quality and friendly service. So far this year we have celebrated New Year's, Lincoln's and Washington's birthdays, St. Patrick's Day and our own two Crazy Days. We know your tips have been greater and that your customers have gotten a big kick out of your creative costumes. Want to do it? Good."

☑ *B/L Recommends:* Set up your own type of crazy, kooky days. Teamwork and cooperation are the real names of your game. Fun and a chance to be a little loose and easy (without going too far) are your objectives. Everyone gains.

One client taught us how to make this type of promotion a success. He encourages everyone to dress in some sort of costume. He takes pictures of everyone and a panel of employees selected from several of his units acts as judges. The winners (always no less than six) receive gift certificates, theater tickets or a free gas fill-up for a car. These periodic *promos help to break monotony and tension*. Bosses, too, can get into the act. Check your calendar. Plan a few fun days. They can't hurt and should help a lot.

Remember When?

Do you remember the last time you were given a free balloon, lollipop, piece of taffy or bubblegum? Boy, *what a thrill to get something for nothing just for being a kid*. Children usually are ignored or, at best, tolerated by most retailers and their employees. We have all heard service people complain about the "little brats." Is this the attitude that you want in your house? Is your operation on the blackball list of the younger generation patronizing your establishment?

☑ *B/L Recommends:* Keep on hand and give away such little items as balloons, bubblegum, lollipops, candies, plastic toys, and rings. Do not believe that fast fooders and franchised coffee shop operators are the only ones allowed to recognize the value of family repeat business. Children have fantastic memories. They can remember exactly when and where they were treated kindly. They will cause their parents to pass up your competition to drive to your establishment—if you have given them good reason to remember your place.

Your hardest task, once you have implemented a system, will be to keep after your employees to follow your instructions. They can't be bothered. Remind them what it is to be a kid. To a child the thought is the thing—not the cost.

And, *do not forget your adult customers*. You can give them sweet-tooth items such as mints and breath fresheners. You can use a small souffle cup as a holder for such items and deliver them as a nice finishing touch when presenting the check. To be different is to be better than your competition. Check the sales of your five-cent mints at your cashstand before you say you cannot afford to give some away. Many guests take them, and your employees definitely do without paying. To increase customer count, make more friends, and encourage repeat business from children of all ages is your business: your most important job.

As Fresh and Clean as a Newborn Babe

What can be more precious to a mother than her child? A parent may do whatever he or she wants with his or her kids, but woe to others who may abuse them. Foodservice operators have recognized their responsibilities to the younger set for years. Complete chains have been built on the family-and-child business. Operators supply booster seats, high chairs, special menus, smaller portions and prices, and free gifts and premiums to attract their young patrons.

Parents and relatives need to know where to dine when they have children in their party. They do not want to be embarrassed, inconvenienced, or have to pay too much for foods that are not suitable. We know that children have a great deal of influence in deciding where the family will eat, and that the family unit will return where the offspring are truly welcome.

We often speak of dirty restrooms repulsing our guests. Well *what of our dirty high chairs?* We have seen some that appear never to have been cleaned. The old grease, stains, and general crud that has been allowed to accumulate on high chairs is certainly unsightly, unsanitary, and unappetizing.

☑ *B/L Recommends:* It is the little things that count with parents. Show them you care about cleanliness and convenience for their children. We encouraged one family-oriented restaurant chain to demonstrate more vividly than their competitors that they love their young customers. Bus persons are required to remove high chairs from the dining room after each use to clean them thoroughly. *They are to wrap the top of the tray* with a plastic (Saran-type) wrap. The wrap stays on till the high chair is delivered to the table or booth. One busperson added his own variation: He places two saltine cracker packets under the plastic wrap so the child will immediately have something to play with and eat. The comments from the parents, as you can imagine, have been excellent. We also recommend that the footrest portion be removed. This is where crackers and crumbs often accumulate. There is also less noise. Kids cannot kick them with their feet. If you want the family trade, show that you know how to care for it.

"The Check Please"

Our guests probably utter this one phrase more than any other. Service personnel are generally trained to be alert to the glance, hand gesture, or verbal request that signifies the patron wants to pay and leave. And usually the service person will respond as quickly as possible to present the correctly totaled guest check. The transaction between the guest and the house is almost at an end. But *how* the guest check is placed before the guest should be a matter of great importance to owners and managers. Will it be presented with class and distinction befitting a smart dinner house, or will it be allowed to lie flat and uninterestingly on a tray emblazoned with the name "Bankamericard"?

Let us assume that your offer of a total eating experience, from the reception area and dining room to the decor, table service, and other accoutrements is worthy of your unique menu, quality of foods, and prices. And your finishing touch—your signature, if you will, is your guest check. Do you present it properly? Do your people know how to present it? Or, do they tentatively slide it between the salt and pepper shakers and the sugar bowl? Why not give them something of which they can be proud. Present your checks with a flourish.

☑ *B/L Recommends:* Fulfill your promise to your guests. Help them to finish their meals in keeping with your grand style. Do not deflate the moment with just any old tired method for the presentation of the guest check, the collection of money and/or credit cards. Create your own gimmick. Your decor or concept is the key. For example: a Chinese or Japanese house could present its checks in an oriental lacquered box. English Pubs or German style restaurants could use beer mugs, steins, or serving trays purchased from English or German breweries. Italian restaurants have bread baskets and wine holders. French restaurants could use wooden cooking bowls, a serving omelette pan, and so forth. A common variety cigar box can be fun also, and create good mention from your guests. And not to be outdone, thoughtful restaurateurs add the extra touch of class by serving a souffle cup of mints, a candy or two, toothpicks, a fresh rose for the ladies, an extra packet of matches, a business card with a note of appreciation handwritten and signed by the owner or maitre d'. Doesn't it make sense to end a great evening of eating pleasure with a more memorable method of exchange before your guests are allowed to leave your house?

This Menu Shed No Light

The design of the store's new menu was a joy to contemplate. Excellent artwork, tasteful type selection, good combination of secondary colors. *It had everything going for it except effectiveness*. The artist worked in well-lit surroundings, so did the printer. The menu proofs were okayed by the owner in an equally bright office. But when the menu was placed in the intimately-lit dining room, guests complained that they couldn't read it. It embarrassed a lot of older patrons who needed good light or large type to read a menu. The subdued lighting also washed out the menu's secondary color tones, and this led to more confusion. A costly re-do was necessary.

☑ *B/L Recommends:* Never select ink, paper or artwork for a new menu without closely studying what effect the lighting in the dining room will have on the completed job. Give first priority to customer needs. Artistic gewgaws sometimes take prizes. A practical menu always produces profits.

Ethics Are an Essential Part of the Menu

There are individuals in this business who seem to look on repeat business as some form of insult. You can tell who these folks are by the way they price their menus. The "extra larges," "supers," and "king sizes" all are priced higher, *ounce for ounce*, than the regular-size portions. Blatantly advertising this little swindle on the menu irks customers who are trying to be careful with their money. It would be less obvious to simply hire a pickpocket for the premises. Much data support the notion of pricing king sizes at a *lesser* per-ounce price. Going the other route provides data to support the truth-in-menu forces.

☑ *B/L Recommends:* Do what we do. When we come across a short changer, we tell him about it. And, it is short changing when somebody deliberately delivers less for more money. *The practice hurts the industry.* We told a big money client this same thing recently. He didn't like it, but he did listen, reluctantly. It's not that we would rather be right than rich. The plain fact is that when ethics are lacking, the void is filled by stringent government regulations.

What Price Jealousy?

We asked the owner of the troubled unit why his coffee carried such a high menu price. "That's what they are getting for it just down the street," he replied. Some other menu items carried stiff prices, too. It's okay, said the owner. "Everybody in town is getting the same prices." This last comment told us the operator had fallen into a trap that snares many restaurant people. He was basing his menu prices on jealousy instead of good sense. The competing store down the street was getting 50¢ for a cup of coffee. Only they were not getting it very often. Everybody in town was asking about $2.10 for a waffle—they were doing a lot more asking than selling as a result.

☑ *B/L Recommends:* Avoid jealousy in menu pricing. *We know of locations that have literally gone out of business because of this practice.* Not only does this failing cut into volume, but it makes a shambles of food cost controls. Once menu items are priced by avarice instead of logic, it is difficult and costly to turn things around.

Banking Hours: 8:55 a.m. to 3:05 p.m.

All of us have waited at the door of a bank, at 8:55 in the morning wishing for once that they would open 5 minutes early. And, haven't most of us rushed to a bank at 3:01 in the afternoon hoping their clock might be slow so we might be allowed in? Here we are: *we are the customers,* yet we are only invited to patronize our favorite banks between the precise hours of nine and three and perhaps till six p.m. on Fridays.

Bank employees seem to enjoy their little opening and closing games. Our watches are never correct. One would think their clocks are set by the U.S. Naval Observatory. Press your nose to the window; plead that you must have change to open your restaurant. Most bank employees would not admit their grandmothers a minute early. They are not paid to care. They believe we need them more than they need us. Of course, they are wrong, but we know we will receive the same treatment elsewhere, so what is the use of our changing banks? It most certainly is a different story with our foodservice customers, or is it?

☑ **B/L Recommends:** Do not treat your guests the same way bankers treat us. Let us say your schedule calls for your employees to be prepared to open your operation at 7:00 a.m. and close at midnight. Why not be different: better, and more considerate of your customers? Do not change your "hours" sign. Train your help to open at 6:55 a.m. and close at 12:05 a.m. The extra five minutes on each end of your hours of operation will make little difference to your personnel or to your schedule. But, the difference will mean a great deal to your customers. The extending of a bit of courtesy can be just one of those little things that will separate your place from your competition. Why not try it? Most of the time we complain that we cannot use our time effectively. Here is an opportunity to put time to work for us. Convince your opening and closing crews to try your *five-minute courtesy plan*. Or you can continue to allow your people to use their banker-type snobbish attitude to keep your guests waiting out in the cold and dark for those extra five minutes. After all, they are only your customers.

Profiting from Waiter/Waitress Sales

Each major industry in the country has a sales force. Nothing happens until the sales force writes the orders. This is a fact of business life. A lot of high-paid executive attention is devoted to how well the sales force handles this vital task. The restaurant industry is about the only exception. No other business in the nation is so casual about the performance of its sales force.

Let's look at how closely the function of a waiter or waitress parallels that of a commercial salesperson: A salesperson writes the order—so does a waiter or waitress. A salesperson looks after customer satisfaction—so does a waiter or waitress. A salesperson earns a commission based on product sales—so does a waiter or waitress.

While waiters and waitresses duplicate the important functions performed by sales people everywhere, they are indoctrinated and trained to perform like menials out of the sixteenth century.

Small wonder the general public regards the serving craft as being at the low end of the social scale. The opinion is daily reinforced by contact with uninterested, poorly indoctrinated people who feel they are more or less trapped in nowhere jobs. The paradoxical part of this is that modern-day serving personnel carry out their chores in food emporiums that cost upward of half a million dollars to put in business. And these servers are the only company representatives that have meaningful communications with customers.

In an average coffee shop, a serving person will write more than $50,000 in business each year. It works out to about $200 a day. Management is content since they have been conditioned not to expect anything better. The store remains in business and delivers, hopefully, a modest six percent pre-tax profit on volume.

What happens if you turn this serving person into a sales-motivated waiter or waitress? The first visible sign is an increase of about 10 percent in sales he or she personally writes. On the surface it appears a minor achievement, hardly worth the attention of management.

After all, he or she is only contributing $20 to daily volume and adding perhaps three dollars to his or her income from tips. *Take a closer look*. His or her contribution to store *profits* goes up over 50 percent due to the dynamics peculiar to our business. In a store operating in the 6 percent profit range here's what happens . . .

The waitress or waiter's 10 percent increase in written sales occurs in a "captive climate," a near-ideal situation from the standpoint of profits. The extra products sold cost little more than the ingredients used in preparation. All the costs for wages, utilities, rent and so on, are incurred up front. Thus, a serving person who cannot sell produces a 6 percent profit for the company. A motivated waiter or waitress brings in over 9 percent on a very modest volume increase.

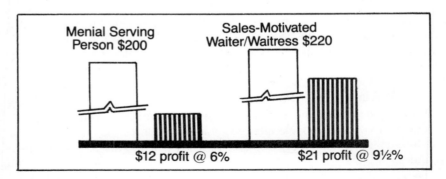

Menial Serving Person $200 — Sales-Motivated Waiter/Waitress $220

$12 profit @ 6% $21 profit @ 9½%

This changed approach increases profits in other tangible and intangible areas. When a waitress or waiter's prestige and income are increased, absenteeism and turnover costs are reduced. As he or she becomes more attuned and responsive to customer requirements, the customers return more frequently. Less reliance has to be placed on expensive advertising campaigns. More productive and precise labor scheduling is possible.

There is nothing startlingly new about this concept. Knowledgeable restaurateurs have been aware of the potential for some time.

It does not require an outrageous expense to increase profitability via improved sales. What is necessary is a dedication to the effort. Four preliminary steps must be accomplished:

A) *Define what you want.* If you want a skilled sales force, even the routine tasks a waiter or waitress performs must be regarded as supportive to the sales and customer satisfaction requirements.

B) *Indoctrinate the entire staff to this philosophy.* Cooks, for example, have to understand that the product they produce must guarantee customer satisfaction. A product that a waitress or waiter cannot sell is worse than useless, it is an affront to the entire organization.

C) *Motivate the service force.* Increased customer sales are not made by mandate of the manager. They are fostered by motivation. The basic motivating factor is increased tip income. Meetings, individual conferences, and incentives stressing the sales theme must be programmed.

D) *Educate the service force.* The waiter or waitress has only a few seconds to obtain the customer's rapport, confidence and trust. Making these seconds count takes training.

ADVERTISING
AND PUBLIC RELATIONS

*There is no influence in business
so valuable as a kind voice,
no stock in the store
that equals in influence
a friendly smile,
no price that has so much pulling power
as dependable service,
and no advertising as far reaching
as the square deal.*

7

ADVERTISING AND PUBLIC RELATIONS

"Advertising and Public Relations" is an expense item on your profit and loss statement. This catchall category may represent an expenditure of anywhere from one to five percent of your gross sales—no small item. Your ad/P.R. budget must include everything from help wanted ads to television.

Work in this area is unlike any other that you perform. You cannot flip a switch as with your utilities and hope things will light up. You must plan precisely where you will spend money, and how much you can afford to spend to increase sales, customer count, and profits. Interestingly, when things are going well, most operators give credit to superior quality and service. But should volume dip, owners often complain that their advertising isn't pulling results.

You may be an excellent and professional restaurateur or hotelier and yet not truly be aware of the many pitfalls that daily await you in this vital area of your business. The ideas that follow are offered to you in the hope that they will make you think carefully and plan ahead whenever you advertise.

Community Economics Need Close Study

Community economics is not a subject generally taught in restaurant management courses. It should be. It is very important to know the amount and source of dollars flowing into your trading area. Here's an idea of what we mean: Generally, every manufacturing job creates anywhere from four to six support jobs. These are activities carried on outside the manufacturing plant. The outside jobs range from subassembly employment to supermarket checking. Now, if there were a labor strike at the plant near your operation, you might think, well, that's not too serious since it only involves 300 workers and not many of them come into the place anyway. But, that's wrong. *The strike has a direct impact on probably 1,500 people*. It reduces the number of discretionary dollars available to them and it is going to affect your operation. Your business depends on discretionary dollars, money that does not have to be spent for necessities and taxes. This type of money also dries up in a community when a manufacturer loses a large government contract.

A client once insisted that we fly halfway across the country to try and find out what was happening at one of his dinner houses. The unit had not done any business to speak of for five weeks. Yet the house was managed by one of the chain's top men. They had poured money into advertising and special promotions, nothing worked. We located the reason on the cab ride in from the airport. A tremendous proportion of the homes in the community had "For Sale" signs on the front lawns. A large defense supplier in an adjacent city suddenly had a prime contract canceled. The manager ran a sharp store. Unfortunately, he locked himself into the back end of his unit. *He really did not know his customers*. He'd heard something about the loss of some contract, but hell, that was in a different town.

☑ *B/L Recommends:* When volume takes a sudden drop, the first thing to do is try and locate the reason. Do not start throwing advertising dollars around in hopes of changing the situation. If your store checks out A-okay, then the reason for depressed volume is probably external in origin. Check the date the volume slide started with back issues of the local newspaper. Consult the local chamber of commerce. People do not print money in their garages, at least most of them don't. They get their money from some primary source. *You have to know what that source is and how much of your volume is dependent upon it*. Then you want to keep track of the financial health of that primary source.

Look Before You Launch That Ad Campaign

Newspaper advertising that does not pay off carries an extra hidden cost. There is no way to recover the time that was lost while the effort was going down the tubes. *That is why advance planning is important*. Too often ad plans are formulated based solely on what the store wants to do. Little or no thought is given to how to transmit the message in order to obtain the best results. Thus, an ad breaks for a dinner special, and right next to it is a competitor's ad for almost the same item at a lower price. When this happens, the ad carrying the higher price endorses that of the competition. Or the ad size may be wrong for the time span in which it appears. A small space ad can be overwhelmed and lost in a page carrying two or three big-space attractions.

☑ *B/L Recommends: Do a little market study before placing your advertising insertion order.* Go to the newspaper office and tell the librarian you want to review restaurant advertising in some back editions. Study what has been done in the past.

Pay particular attention to the periods in which you plan to do your heaviest advertising in the future. Look for consistent patterns in your competitors' ads in those time frames. Go back over a three- to four-year span and check on a repeat ad placed by a competitor. This will tell you two things: (A) The ad will most likely be repeated in the future; (B) It has a history of pulling satisfactory results within the newspaper's circulation area. With this information, you are better prepared to produce an advertising effort of your own with greater appeal and impact.

A Lean Scene

Shortages of gasoline have an effect on all types of business. Businesses whose customers travel to reach them are hit especially hard. Prudent business owners should take heed. When gasoline is in short supply, so are customers for those restaurants that do peak volume during summer months.

☑ *B/L Recommends:* Do some contingency planning. If it looks like tourist business is going to be thin, *beef up local advertising and promotion.* Develop new menu specials and price one or two low enough to be a strong attraction to local customers. Create tie-ins with community events in a big way.

Try Mapping for More Traffic

There's a big sign outside the restaurant. The place has been in business for years. A lot of traffic rolls by the doors every day. Therefore, *the entire town knows the location of the store.* Right?

☑ *B/L Recommends:* Never make that assumption. Turnover in American communities averages around 17 percent per year. In your ads, promise 'em good food and service, *but give 'em a simple map.* Any large space classified phone directory should feature a map. Take a tip from the realtors; they know how important maps are in building traffic at a site. When take-out business is being featured in an ad, a map is almost as vital as a description of the foods available.

Wave at 'Em to Get Attention

In the newspaper business, they are called tombstone ads. They appear month after month the same size in the same place in the same publication. The ads don't really sell tombstones. *In fact, they don't sell much of anything.* Publishers love them. Tombstone ad schedules bring in a lot of bucks. That's not the case for the advertisers trying to sell their food and services. People get so used to seeing the ad saying the same thing in the same place in the paper that they actually do not see it at all. Repetition of this sort is very expensive, since you are paying out money for something that is not bringing in a commensurate return.

☑ *B/L Recommends:* If you want customers, "wave" at them. A wave advertising schedule means you use the same amount of money as a tombstone schedule. But you use a large-size ad one time, then, draw back and build up the budget before you run again. *The theory is, you want to attract new, regular customers*. If you have to advertise regularly just to bring in one-time customers, your operation is in jeopardy. Therefore, a wave schedule is more efficient than a tombstone schedule.

Discretionary income in a community, which is what restaurants live on, varies from week to week. At the first of the month it is high, since this is payday for most folks. It drops, then goes up a little in the middle of the month. A wave ad schedule can be used to attract more attention when people have the most money to spend. It can also be used to outshout the competition when there are fewer dollars around to attract. Either way, it is better to have your ad waving at people than lying quietly on the page, resting in peace.

Take a Page From Your Local Supermarket

Read your local newspaper's food section—you know, the one with three-quarter and full-page ads that list all the supermarket items, prices, and departments. Every advertisement always pushes one or more items from each category or department in the store, such as liquor, frozen foods, produce, groceries, baked goods, and meat. Every ad tells its readers that there are values for everyone—all the time. They do not advertise one meat or canned food special. They advertise in such a way as to gain the widest possible appeal. Can't we in foodservice take a hint from supermarket mass merchandisers?

☑ *B/L Recommends:* We did. We encouraged a coffee shop chain to *advertise its complete food menu*. You, too, can run a condensed version or reprint of your menu. You will be amazed at the number of customers who will read it at their leisure, come into your store, and compliment you for telling them of the variety and prices which you offer. Haven't we all been told by our regular customers that they did not know that we sold certain foods—even though they have been patronizing our restaurants for years?

Faddy Ads Are Bad

The advertising business gets swept by fads just as the restaurant industry does. Currently, ad artists are wild about laying heavy horizontal black bars at the top and bottom of ads. The presentation is strong when the ads appear separately. The trouble comes when the ads are stacked on a newspaper page. *The bars link the ads together.* Whoever is on the bottom is a loser in this layout combination.

☑ *B/L Recommends:* Insist that your ads carry attractive full borders. Check tear sheets to be sure your ad is not linked to some other product on the page by a look-alike border.

Consider using slanted headlines in your copy. Very few restaurant ads do this. A slanted headline may take a bit more space, but it stands out and attracts more attention.

Yum, Fleas Fricassee, Cockroaches a la Carte

How about dinner tonight in a place that advertises itself in big bold print as a "Pestaurant"? It's a specialized supper house, as you might suspect. Actually, the house attraction is not insects; the bugs are in the ad copy. Over a half-million newspaper readers will have a chance to see the ad. It will not be noticed by all of them, *just the ones looking for a place to dine out*. Why do guys who would rather jump in a Fryolater than serve one bad meal, let shabby advertising poison thousands of potential guests? The ad agency, which did the work, will probably offer to pay for the goof. They should. It still will not cover the irreparable harm done to the business.

☑ *B/L Recommends:* One person, in-house, must have responsibility for final proof approval of all ad copy. *Never delegate this function to an outside vendor.* You do not accept product deliveries with your eyes closed. Why do it with advertising? The reputation of the house for quality and excellence rides on what appears in print as well as on the plate.

Good Use for Imprinted Cups

Do you use any imprinted paper or plastic cups in your operation? If you do, you might consider an unusual use that has proven quite successful.

☑ *B/L Recommends:* Select nearby businesses that can complement your food operation. Gas stations, doctors' offices, retailers, motels, garages, and other locations that regulars and tourists might frequent are good places to try this trick: Give a half or full tube of your imprinted disposable cups to these business friends. Ask them to give one *empty* cup to their customers, explaining that they can have it filled with coffee at your place free of charge or with purchase. Everyone will be the beneficiary of this goodwill gesture, and you will be the greatest beneficiary of all for initiating it and handling these new guests as graciously as possible. This will also encourage some very nice word-of-mouth advertising.

No Malpractice Here

Many of us wish we could retrieve the hundreds and thousands of dollars that we foolishly spent on advertising through the years. Most of us have learned valuable lessons on how to search for new customers on a budget that we can afford. But we always seem to feel that our best customers must come from far away and we *neglect our local friends and customers*.

☑ *B/L Recommends:* Establish yourself in your community as the best, most friendly place to patronize. *Create positive word-of-mouth publicity.* For instance, you can approach the doctors and dentists in your neighborhood.

Supply them with cards that they can personalize with the name of their young patients to receive a free ice cream cone, food or beverage in your establishment. Contact local retailers such as shoe stores and bicycle shops. They will be happy to be nice to their young children, especially if it does not cost them a cent. You can control how many cards are given away by the doctors and retailers. Give out a few at first. Secretly "key" the cards with initials or numbers so you can spot where they came from to determine just who is cooperating with you. These doctors and retailers, by the nature of this promotion, will be using their influence to encourage people to patronize your store.

Some Clues on Couponing

Couponing is a practice newspaper advertising representatives love to promote. An effective coupon ad usually requires more space than a normal display ad. But results can be disappointing.

We encountered two problem situations in one short period. One manager was dismayed because the coupons were brought in by the same people each time the advertisement appeared. The other manager emphasized the size of the deal he was offering by printing a big coupon, but received an exceedingly small return.

The first manager had neglected to put the store's address on the coupon, although the address appeared in the ad itself. *Coupon savers normally clip just the coupons;* they do not hold on to the entire ad. The reason the manager was seeing the same faces with the coupons was simple: The old customers knew where the store was located when they decided to use the coupon. New customers did not have the address, so they simply went on the the next coupon offering they had clipped.

The big coupon did not work out because it was too bulky, and *potential users were unfamiliar with the size*. Coupon savers have been conditioned to dollar bill-size coupons by the big food section advertisers. Any deviation from that size lessens the effectiveness of the coupon return.

☑ *B/L Recommends:* If you are going to get into coupon advertising, be sure and *think through the process from the customer's standpoint*. The store address should be on the coupon, and so should an expiration date. The way inflation is going, unexpired coupons can be more of a threat than a promotion. But try to avoid qualifiers such as "before 6:00 p.m.," "Mondays only," or "one per person." These cut into the effectiveness of the ad, and tend to create more confusion than protection.

There is a pattern of returns with coupon ads, if the offer is attractive. The coupon return generally peaks on the third or fourth appearance of the advertisement, and then starts to go down. It is important to keep track of the returns in order to back off from the promotion at the right time and not waste advertising dollars.

Coupon Books Can Put You in Bad Company

Over 90 percent of the best restaurants in town have already signed up for the latest coupon book, the salesman tells you. If you don't sign, he hints darkly, the county will probably by using your dining room for a deer park in a couple of months. It's all nonsense, but it works. Annually, thousands of operators are gulled into signing coupon book agreements. These are deals whereby you get a page of advertising in a book and the benefits of supposedly lavish advertising efforts. All you have to do is put out a two-for-one special each time a coupon comes in the door. *It is not as beneficial or harmless as it sounds*. First of all, your ad in the book may come out printed right, or it may not. Whatever restrictions, such as an expiration date, you place on coupon redemptions may appear, or may not. You are not the only with the problem. Everybody in the book is faced with the same situation. The outfits that print these books have been known to be a little careless, just the same as the sales representatives that write up the ads. Some operators find they can't live with the deal as it appears in print, and they then refuse to redeem the coupons.

The most eager group to get into coupon books are those with marginal stores. It gives them advertising they cannot afford. By the time the books are published, many of the marginal operators have moved on to other pastures. The new owners of the businesses, since they had no part in the coupon deal, usually refuse redemption, as do the people with the misprinted ads. The books, of course, are peddled to the public at a substantial price tag. When coupon users start getting burned by redemption refusals, *you are damned for the company you keep*, regardless of whether you are carrying out the agreement in good faith or not. Coupon deals are also the bane of franchisors. One franchisee goes for a deal, the other refuses it. The coupon customer doesn't check the address too closely so he or she gets turned away and turned off to the entire chain.

Non-redemption is only one of the problems inherent in coupon book promotions. Regardless of the local sponsorship, these coupon packages are put together by teams of professionals traveling from one city to the next. When an operator is signed on the dotted line, they ask for good faith deposits, or try to sell a lot of worthless promotional "extras."

☑ *B/L Recommends:* Establish a firm policy on coupons. *Only permit placement in recognized local media*. Never allow your coupons to appear in bad company. If you tell sales representatives that up front, you'll have more time to devote to your business and you'll have happier customers.

Hello, Big Boy . . . Come Up and See Me Sometime

Mae West became famous for this great one-liner when she gave her suitors the message that she was inviting them to visit her in her apartment. We in foodservice can attract people who live in their apartments to come down (or up) to see us in our establishments. Customers like us to be different, too.

☑ *B/L Recommends:* Today's high-rise apartments and commercial buildings literally tower over many of our restaurants and smaller buildings. Tenants usually have an excellent view of the surrounding area that often includes a great view of our rooftops and equipment. There's the key, *your rooftop.* Use it to your advantage. We accepted one such challenge. We painted a large sign and mounted it at an angle so that the tenants living and working in the apartments and offices above could read it. The sign was an extension of the personality of the restaurant. It was friendly and brief. It gave the phone number and name of the owner. He received excellent word-of-mouth comment and publicity from this stunt. Do not hesitate to use a bit of humor either, as you turn your rooftop into your own *outdoor billboard.* Great advertising, low cost—high return.

How Old Are Your "New" Signs?

The words "new" and "now" promise guests an unusual or different eating experience. But what if the signs, tabletalkers or menu clip-ons are tattered and dog-eared from prolonged use? What type of promise do they make to your guests?

☑ *B/L Recommends:* Take a critical look at your outside signs and banners. Check all interior advertising. Do these units look as new as the print proclaims? If not, remove them, *customers readily spot these kinds of false promises.* It makes them suspicious of everything on the menu.

Under New Management

It's a bannered statement you see all the time. "Under New Management" is about the most worthless statement a restaurant can make about itself. So what if the store has new management? Was the old management bad? Is the new management experienced enough to make things better? There is simply nothing positive in this type of impersonal message. Yet non-thinking operators and franchise companies constantly try to make it work.

☑ *B/L Recommends:* In a transition situation, be better and be different. Don't disparage or allude to the previous management—that's what you do with the word "new" in the message. *Instead, invite the public in the meet a specific person, by name.* Advertise that "Joe Jones is here to meet you," or "Come on in and meet Joe Jones." List Joe's top credentials, too.

Community Communications Have New Importance

If you think Big Brother isn't busy forcing his whims on us citizens, look around for a restaurant in some of our newer, super-regulated communities. *You can't tell a hamburger handout from a bank or a mortuary.* Row upon row of brown boxy structures reflect the bareness of the bureaucratic mind. The only distinguishing marks are the outside signs. The signs themselves are being squeezed down to insignificance. Whole towns are starting to look as though the building plans were borrowed from a commune in North Korea. We watched one of the country's more celebrated hamburger chains gamble $300,000 in one such California town. The store, on a good corner location, was open for three weeks. Volume was terrible. Most of the identifying characteristics, which originally made the chain so successful, were stripped from the outside of the building. The zealots on the city planning commission did leave the store with a fair-sized reader board sign. But the chain's management had a lot to learn about doing business under highly restrictive conditions. In all the time the store was open the only message transmitted to the community via the board was "Hot 'n Juicy Hamburgers."

☑ *B/L Recommends:* Community communications are always important. When a store has to assume the same drabness as every other business in the area, *good community communications are vital*. A reader board that does not carry sprightly, frequently changed messages is as enticing as a tombstone. Reader boards are designed as a means of communication. If a reader board is confined to the transmission of a single, weary advertising slogan, its potential is sadly wasted.

Teenage Trade Needs Deft Handling

Teenage customers, who wants them? Not too many restaurants, that's for sure. A lot of veteran managers are still haunted by incidents that happened in the riotous 60's. This standoffish attitude toward teenage trade is nearly always reflected by the manager's employees. But teenagers move into adulthood rather rapidly, and they do not quickly forget a gratuitous snub by a waitress, or a dining experience in a suspicious, near-hostile atmosphere. We are not attempting to make a case for another of society's downtrodden groups, all we are saying is that deliberately discouraging teenage customers is not good business in the long run.

☑ *B/L Recommends:* Try and see that teenagers get the same exact treatment accorded adult customers. It isn't easy. Teenagers are subject to unusual peer pressures and this makes for erratic behavior. It is a good idea to discuss this topic with employees. If the staff members understand the cause, they are more capable of coping with the effects.

Rumors Are Treacherous Things

The health department had never shut the store down. Yet there was a freely circulating rumor around town that it had. The business was being hurt as a result. When management first heard the rumor, they shrugged it off. It didn't go away, and things became serious. Tracing the rumor was an arduous task.

The difficulty had begun when management elected to cut back the number of hours the store was operational at night. *The logic was sufficient, the execution was poor*. The new hours were duly posted on the door panel.

The hours sign was small and could not be seen when the lights were off and the store closed. The big, "Sorry, We're Closed" sign in the window was highly visible. As near as could be learned, the rumor was born when a square dance club arrived late one night and found the premises dark. One of the party loudly and caustically observed, "Ha, the health department must have shut'em down." It was quickly edited and transmitted at "The health department shut'em down." Despite clear evidence the store was open daily, many people in the community "knew for a fact" the health department had to shut down the store.

☑ *B/L Recommends:* Any time you hear a rumor about your business, treat it seriously. Try to trace the source. *There could we be some basis for whatever slander is in circulation.* What happened in the instance above, was caused by a communication failure between management and the store's customers. Management did not clearly proclaim the new hours, and the disappointed customers formed their unfavorable and erroneous conclusions as to why the store was closed. It was almost as bad as if the health department *had* sealed off the place.

Clip Joints Can Have News for You

Restaurant consulting requires us to get a lot of haircuts. It is more a business tactic than an obsession with neatness. When stores have problems, owners want answers in a hurry. If the difficulty seems keyed to something other than staff malfeasance, *the local barbershop can usually supply a few clues.* At one barbershop we were told how to make a black-market buy on the same quality of steaks as served in a high ticket restaurant on the next block. In a different place, we learned that another store was serving only horsemeat (untrue, but that was the word being passed in the community). Once, when we were working with the foodservice of a famous racetrack, a barber told us how a new tout scam was operating. Even the track's security service was surprised. And we also found out that one store manager had made a slurring remark against some craftsmen. Their union headquarters was up the street from the restaurant. Over 1,200 members heard of the comment and were justifiably angered.

☑ *B/L Recommends:* When you need local business intelligence, try a trip to the barbershop. *There is a knack to picking up the information.* Do not go to one of those fancy frou-frou parlors. Pick a good workaday shop. Be casual. Ask your important questions only after a couple of friendly general inquiries. *Never argue or take issue with the replies.* You want information, not a debate. Be grateful for the barber's wisdom. He expects a tip. The more he feels he can put you under obligation, the more information he is inclined to supply. Keep in mind that the intelligence may not be accurate, but it is in circulation in the community.

ESTABLISHING
MANAGEMENT POLICIES

I wondered why somebody
didn't do something—
then I realized
I was somebody.

8

ESTABLISHING MANAGEMENT POLICIES

Policy-making is the most valuable prerogative of management. It can make the rules by which the game of business is to be played—what power!

An owner, president, franchisee, supervisor, or manager can establish almost any policies he or she may wish. Enforcement, however, is a vastly different story. It is, therefore, most desirable to develop policies that fit logically into the makeup of one's system and into the pattern that has been set up to achieve all objectives.

We all need rules to live and work. "Standard operating procedures" is just a fancy phrase for such regulations on how a business is to be operated. We most certainly want our people to know what they are *not* to do. But policies can also be extremely positive in nature, if we choose to develop and approach everything from the right side of things.

This section on S.O.P. (standard operating procedures) describes both negative and positive examples. It may give you many new ways to approach difficult situations that will aid you in developing better teamwork and better compliance with your rules.

Confusion = Unhappy Guests and Lost Sales

The concepts "portion control" and "standard operating procedures" may strike you and your personnel as being too bothersome to worry about, but *your customers certainly appreciate them.* One case in particular drove the point home to a director of operations of a large chain when he replaced a manager, who was on vacation, with a new man. The regular manager is what you might call a "front of the house" man. He is not a kitchen man. He hates to cook and get his hands dirty. He hires cooks and expects them to do the cooking.

The vacation man is just the opposite. He realizes his cooks need occasional assistance and like to see someone in management who cares about their work.

We were fortunate to be with him in the galley when a guest check was presented by a worried waitress. Written across the check was, "I have been a good customer of yours for years. I always eat eggs and potatoes, but if you keep reducing the portion of potatoes, I will go elsewhere." We immediately checked the plates and set-up instructions that the line cooks were following. Sure enough, they were using eight-inch plates in place of five-inch plates for a side order of hash brown potatoes. Visually, what may fit quite naturally on a five-inch plate can appear very small on a larger one. We checked other food and plate dimensions and also found that oversized portions were being served on overly large dishes. The temporary manager was stymied: should he come down real hard on the cooks, ignore the problem, or correct it? He was instructed to gradually bring all items into line to avoid further customer dissatisfaction and, of course, further loss of food.

☑ *B/L Recommends: Crack down hard on the manager (or yourself) who will not wise up to the absolute need for precise portion control and S.O.P.* The size of chinaware and glassware to be used for every menu item must be clearly identified for proper portion control. You will seriously upset your food cost and your guests if your serviceware inventory is short and you have to substitute oversized dishes to fill your orders. Consider too, the difficulties this makes for your service personnel, as they attempt to arm- or tray-carry incorrectly sized dishes. And, when all else fails to impress on you the reasons for perfect portion control, consider your guests and their confusion. They will quit you in a moment if you give them cause to think they have been gypped in your house.

Sidewalks of New York

Most of us have heard of garbage collectors' strikes in some of our major cities. But, have you personally smelled and seen the tremendous buildup of garbage, boxes, bags, cans, paper, and plastic cups? Whew! A mess is never anything to be proud of—especially when it is in front of your own door. What if it were your own door? Would you go along with the mess, or would you try to do something about it? A city-wide strike may be too much to fight by yourself. *However, what of the dirt in front of your restaurant that you can do something about?*

☑ *B/L Recommends:* Do not accept the grime, automobile and pedestrian traffic buildup that accumulates in front of your establishment. We asked one operator to specifically scour and *wash down his front sidewalk each day.* He argued that the dirt would be tracked from his neighbors' sidewalks to his. We insisted that he try it. He did and his customer comments have been most favorable. His super-clean sidewalk has become a standing invitation to guests to enter. Logically, customers conclude that if the operator keeps his front walk so clean, then his restaurant must serve quality foods and that his interior must be impeccably clean—which it is. The thought, extra elbow grease, and soap have proven well worth the effort.

It Stinks!

Do you use your nose in your business? Your customers sure do.

☑ *B/L Recommends:* Be careful with garbage, trash, bleach, ammonia, and other cleaning agents out front where your customers sit or stand. Sharp, pungent aromas disturb customers when they are trying to eat. Medicinal odors are not generally conducive to a pleasant eating experience. Check your day and night crews. Do not allow them to saturate side towels (bar towels) and mops with harsh smelling liquids and detergents to be used in your dining rooms and customer areas while you are still open for business. Too often have we seen buspersons and dishwashers mopping down aisles next to customers who are eating. True, eventually the smells will go away—and so may your customers.

Keeping Your Company's History

It can be a useful business tool, it can make a wonderful keepsake, but *most of the time it never gets a chance to be either one*. Scrapbooks that could tell a company's history are usually sadly neglected items.

☑ *B/L Recommends:*Maintain a scrapbook. Divide it into two sections, one for pictures and newspaper clippings about the company, the other section for advertising clips. *Pictures of parties and banquets make good sales tools when discussing future group bookings*. They illustrate your skill in putting together banquet and party programs. Pictures also sell profitable extra features.

Whatever has been said about the company, good or bad, should also be pasted in the book, always with the appropriate date. The favorable material acts as your goodwill barometer. It shows the status of the restaurant in a community. The *unfavorable items can be used in orienting new employees*. To illustrate the importance of keeping the back door locked, one company made it a point to show all new employees a scrapbook picture of a night crew being released from the walk-in after a stickup. They never had a repeat of the problem.

On the advertising side, each time a new ad appears, a copy should go into the book along with the schedule, the costs, and later, an evaluation of the effectiveness of the campaign. Be sure to include the telephone classified directory clipping in this section. This part of the scrapbook is a great aid in planning future promotions and making advertising purchases.

The Black Book

We have yet to meet an owner or manager who would admit that he or she lacks good communications skills. Yet, every day in the foodservice industry, instructions are garbled or misinterpreted—*sometimes intentionally*. In many cases, day shifts don't leave word for night shifts. Night shifts do not communicate with day shifts. No record was made when, for a perfectly valid reason, somebody strayed from approved systems and procedures. There is no continuity in the record of unusual occurrences.

☑ *B/L Recommends:* Every restaurant should have, and use, a "day-at-a-glance" desk date book. Used properly, it becomes a unit diary. Management enters days-off given; overtime authorized; suppliers contacted; work in progress; disciplinary problems; *names and phone numbers of customers with problems;* who said what, and to whom, and at what time. It could be the most valuable book on the premises.

Scheduling of Personnel

Ever consider that management is frequently responsible for fouling up the work (labor) schedules of its employees? Non-thinking or lazy managers often leave random notes for personnel to "find" with their names and shifts written on them. Should employees not find or in any way misunderstand their schedules, they will invariably guess incorrectly and fail to show up on their proper shifts. Are not customers and other personnel too valuable to foul up?

☑ *B/L Recommends:* Use common sense and a simple 25¢ blue and red pencil. Select one and only one spot in your store, be it the bulletin board, a place near your time clock, or an area in the rear that the majority of your personnel must pass, as the permanent place for all work schedules. Next, write all schedules clearly specifying full names, telephone contact numbers, daily and weekly shifts, uniform sizes (if necessary), and your own special code words for their specific duties such as: (W) Waitress, (H-C) Hostess-Cashier, (C-BU) Cook, Back-up, (BU-D) Back-up, Dishwasher, (Bus) Busperson, etc. Use a blue pencil to indicate all a.m. shifts and a red pencil to specify all p.m. shifts to avoid confusion. Remember, 7-3, 8-12, 9-1, could easily be misunderstood to mean a.m. or p.m. shifts. Managers have a responsibility to communicate as precisely as possible the exact hours they want their people to work. To insure proper communication, have employees initial their schedules.

Guaranteed to Save You Money

Equipment guarantees and warranties are like insurance policies—they are not needed until something goes wrong. They represent a lot of money, as do insurance policies. We seldom visit a restaurant that keeps its equipment warranties readily at hand. *We have never found anyone in authority with any idea when a guarantee expires on any piece of equipment.* It is difficult to understand the logic behind spending thousands of dollars on equipment then not spending a few minutes trying to protect the investment.

☑ *B/L Recommends:* Establish a file folder for each piece of equipment in the store. The folder should contain the instruction manual and warranty. Make sure all required postcards needed to establish guarantee eligibility have been mailed to the manufacturer. On the outside of each folder write the expiration date of the guarantee. Tab and file alphabetically by the manufacturer's name. This is so the nameplate on the equipment can be easily matched with the file data. *Mark your wall calendar with expiration dates.* This will remind you to call for factory authorized service just before the guarantee expires. Make sure you get your money's worth.

Door Stoppers for Sale . . . Special $19.84

Heck, most of us cannot be bothered with those triangular rubber door stoppers or wedges of wood. Do you realize what some of us use to hold doors open, or as pallets on which to stack merchandise? All too often, we use a carton of merchandise.

☑ *B/L Recommends:* Check your storerooms, walk-in boxes, equipment rooms, and those other areas where you store valuable goods. We did. We checked the purchases of one unit operator and noticed he continued to order one case of product costing $19.84, yet all the while he had been using a case of that merchandise to block open a storeroom door. It does sound a bit ridiculous when you think about it. Do not use cartons of goods for all the wrong purposes.

Buy—Don't Borrow

How often, if you are in an organization with more than one store, have you had to borrow merchandise from your fellow manager's unit, promising to pay them back as soon as you receive your next delivery? How often have others borrowed items from you with a similar promise? And haven't you been disappointed to find that the merchandise was not returned as promised, due to any number of legitimate reasons and poor excuses?

☑ *B/L Recommends:* Borrow if you must! But, to avoid excuses, oversights, forgetfulness on both the part of the lender and the borrower, *purchase* the merchandise outright from the other store. Make out a petty cash paid out, and pay for whatever you need. You know, or should know, the cost of the items you need. In this manner you will be able to maintain control of your own cost-of-sales figure, inventory, and avoid being "86" (out) on certain items that may be crucial to your operation because the other guy forgot to return it.

Are You Positive You Do Not Have Any Negatives?

Develop a fast and efficient system to handle all reorders and drag orders. Teach personnel to fold, mark, and "call in" to cooks and prep people that what is now being ordered is a *rush,* and that the order must go to the front of the line to be processed immediately, with no arguments. *A guest is waiting.*

The Reorder—a positive condition: A guest likes what you have to offer, and wants more of the same, or wishes to order an additional food or beverage to complete the meal. *Your service person has sold something that will increase the check* and make the guest's eating experience a better one, due in part to the effective use of a reorder system. Many a service person has stopped selling because, through a lack of teamwork, what was ordered could not be obtained in time to do any good.

☑ *B/L Recommends:* A reorder system is the mechanical function that makes suggestive selling successful. A guest who decides to order a side of toast with a la carte eggs *does not want the toast after the eggs have been eaten or have turned cold.* A side of fries, a vegetable, dessert, etc., that is needed or sold to complete a meal must be treated as *top priority.*

The Drag Order—a negative condition: A drag order is *possibly the worst thing that your house can inflict on a guest.* Someone has neglected to complete whatever has been ordered. Any lack of teamwork between the back of the house and the front service person can slow turnover and increase customer dissatisfaction. How often do you allow foods to be served to one guest while another in the same party must wait for an order to be corrected, taken away, and returned with the resultant apologies because someone goofed?

☑ *B/L Recommends:* A drag order system must be developed to call immediate attention to the fact that a guest cannot finish a meal because all or some of it is missing. Your menu has promised specific foods and combinations. To neglect to deliver them is wrong. This is a prime reason why service people should check back with their guests to determine if anything is lacking or dragging.

In both instances, reorders and drag orders demand the immediate attention of everyone connected with the preparation and service of whatever has been newly requested or improperly prepared. Your guests cannot finish or leave. *The key to suggestive selling is a reorder system. The key to repeat business is a fast drag order (make good) system.* Teamwork is the answer. Incomplete orders, omissions, and mistakes will happen in any operation. Discuss these vitally important positive and negative conditions with your personnel. Complete cooperation is of primary importance.

Substitutions or "I Didn't Know That"

Ever give any thought to what your customers order, receive, and pay for—and whether they do pay for it? Do you allow any changes from your existing menu? Do your waiters and waitresses or counter personnel give your customers everything they wish? Do your people make such substitutions as cottage cheese for french fries, tomatoes for potatoes, soup for salad, ham for roast beef, a glass of wine for a beverage? How about the portions? What kind of controls have you placed on such changes from your standard operating procedures?

☑ *B/L Recommends:* Immediately ask your waitresses, waiters, counter personnel, and cooks to make up a list of all suggestions, substitutions, and variations they can recall preparing or serving. Next (even if you know all the answers), have them explain the sizes of the portions they have been giving. We said "giving." Ask which items they interchange at no cost; which they do charge for, and how much extra they do assess. Compute your costs, yields, and portion-control quantities. Weigh each item that you serve in combination with other foods versus that which you serve on an a la carte basis, or as a side order. For example: a simple side of french fried potatoes may weigh approximately five ounces, while fries on a combination plate may only scale out at three to three and one half ounces.

We believe you will be quite surprised to learn that many of your help may be charging or giving away your merchandise both incorrectly and inconsistently. Not only may they be all fouled up, but the worst part may be that your customers are confused. It is not at all unusual to learn that customers are receiving substitutions on certain days or shifts at no additional charge, while at other times they either are charged or cannot get the items they wish. Post a list of all substitutions, prices, and preparation instructions for all your personnel to follow—every day, on every shift. And if you do not wish to allow any substitutions, which is your prerogative, that is fine too. Just be consistent.

Care and Control of Freebies

Most operators extend complimentary privileges for food and lodging to special guests for a variety of reasons. Supervisors, partners, public relations people, advertising people, consultants, and family members are just a few that go into the category. *The foods and services they use should be documented, for several important reasons.*

☑ *B/L Recommends:* Few things are more enjoyable than receiving free foods and services in a restaurant. It can be all the more important to the recipients of the complimentary items *if they are aware of the complete retail value.* Do not allow yourself or your people to pick up or okay a "comp" for anyone without the VIP first being allowed to see and *sign* the guest check or receipt. Signing the check enhances the VIP's importance, and the signature acts as a control for the goods given away.

If You Let Them, They'll Give Away the Door Keys

Recently we were with a good-sized dinner party of people not associated with the restaurant business. After serving the entree, the waitress checked back to see if everything was satisfactory. One person in the group felt his steak had not been prepared as requested; everything else was okay. The waitress offered to replace the steak. The guest declined. His unhappiness was not so great as to prevent him from making two trips to the salad bar. He finished all the steak, the baked potato and other accompaniments. *When the check was delivered, the cost of the meal for this slightly unhappy patron was deleted*. The other members of the party thought this was a most hospitable gesture and voted "a big tip for our gracious little waitress."

☑ *B/L Recommends:* Every restaurant must have a policy in force to take care of unhappy customers. But *do not turn policy implementation over to personnel who depend on tips*.

Now Hear This: No Customers Allowed

Shutting down a customer area is a frequent expediency in the life of a restaurant. *However, when an area is closed off, it does not have to be defended to the death by employees*. Despite floor signs, chair barricades, and mop buckets, guests sometimes wander into a closed area. Whether the guest is seeking a restroom or a meal is a matter of indifference to the employee holding his fortified position. The employee proclaims: "You can't come in here—this station is closed!" This embarrasses the guest and next to a primed cannon, is an excellent way to chase him or her off the premises. Herding folks into confined areas as a convenience to employees is an acceptable practice in prisons. It is not a good restaurant public relations tactic.

☑ *B/L Recommends:* Operators must instruct personnel as to which areas are to be closed, re-opened, and secured, if at all. The primary concern should be the guest and his or her comfort. *Labor efficiency is nice; profits are vital*.

The Empty Restaurant

A true scenario in 9 acts, loaded with do's and don'ts:

Act 1   The scene: a million dollar, well known lunch and dinner house on restaurant row with a famous name and reputation for fish and other specialties. A large sign out front advertises, "Open for Lunch." A party of four, with reservation, arrives on time for lunch.

Act 2   Exactly two other tables are occupied with guests. The party of four is seated in a booth by a pleasant hostess, who asks if they wish to order drinks. They reply they will have wine with their lunch. She disappears.

Act 3   The busboy serves the water setups, breads, and an iced butter dish.

Act 4   The waiter arrives several minutes later to inquire if anyone wants to order drinks. The guests repeat their desire for wine. *He* disappears.

Act 5   The place is still not busy. There obviously is no communication between the hostess and the waiter. The guests, still sitting and waiting, request menus.

Act 6   The veteran waiter (an older gentleman) finally returns to take the orders. He neglects to offer a wine list or make suggestions.

Act 7 Waiter delivers the food: two Crab Louie Salads and two other fish entrees. The salads lack imagination and consistent preparation. The only similarity is the high price. The guests request a bottle of wine and midway through their meal receive same.

Act 8 The waiter does not return till the check is requested. The complete meal, because of the slow and inattentive service, takes almost two hours— much too long.

Act 9 The four guests stop talking business and begin to grumble over the poor service and food. They agree they will not return. They leave a minimum tip, pay, and leave. The waiter gives them "the eye" because he has been under-tipped. The hostess is seated on the end stool at the bar, drinking coffee, waiting for new guests to arrive.

☑ *B/L Recommends:* *No restaurant can "let down" for certain meals or periods, and then expect to rise to its glorious heights of quality and service at other times.* No operation can afford to be less than what is promised by its name, menu, decor, and prices. You undoubtedly recognized the above scenes. This stage play, with variations, has had a longer run than *My Fair Lady.* Audiences have disappeared with each showing. Critically, as in our 9-act play, *no one cared about the guests.* The slow motion service, the inconsistency of the food, and the non-communication between the help were all too obvious. The chef, or kitchen manager must have been elsewhere when the foods were prepared. The hostess could not have cared less about her guests. It is conceivable that this young lady was intimidated by the older waiter, who may be stubborn enough to think he can do no wrong—that he knows all there is to know about service. *Just exactly who is to be in charge of the floor?* The waiter or the hostess? The answer must be clearly defined.

The old waiter, bless him, may well remember the days when he personally served such greats as Mary Pickford and Harold Lloyd. But so what? Some people are impressed at being in the company of movie stars, politicians, and other big names. However, most of us cater to the average person who wants a good meal for the money. We cannot afford for our own people to be snobs. Instead of playing to standing room only crowds, some of our restaurants are playing to empty seats.

Foodservice operators agree: *More mistakes are made during their slow periods* than during their rush periods. Why must we continue to accept and even encourage this negative situation? We take cash register readings to define how much we gross during our busy times, and our slow periods. Perhaps we should show more interest in those guests who patronize our establishments during our slow hours than in our readings. Aren't we all guilty of this habit at times?

Sorry Ma'am Those Coupons Have Expired

Pick up a newspaper, magazine, or look at your week's mail and you will find umpteen coupons that have been offered by foodservice establishments from fast-fooders to dinner houses, hotels to resorts. Today, people can select from a wide variety of specials on which to save money. And they just as readily neglect to check the expiration dates on the coupons they save and use. No question about it, coupons with expiration dates are designed to create a sense of urgency. Customers are supposed to come in and buy, or miss the opportunity. However, we have seen cashiers refuse coupons that had expired only a day or two earlier. We dislike situations in which foodservice people can use their authority against their guests.

A good many of us have been improperly influenced by supermarket and drug store merchandisers and their supplier-manufacturers. Manufacturers are hard put to keep their merchandise on the shelves of their retailers. Space is at a premium. They have to keep churning customers to ask for their items in order to keep their items on the shelves.

But we in our restaurants have no such name brands on our shelves. The item we make and sell today will probably be the same that we will be selling in the foreseeable future. And, from time to time, we may feature a sandwich, dinner, or combination plate on a coupon. So what if a customer presents a coupon shortly after an expiration date? It is our customer—past, present, and hopefully, in the future—whom we are trying to please. We are not some distant manufacturer who must sell our products through intermediaries. Our restaurants are the end-sources where the real action is—where the final transaction takes place.

☑ *B/L Recommends:* Take a liberal view of such restrictive policies as they apply to your most valuable assets—your customers. The vast majority of guests who redeem our discounted offers are not transients. Most are regulars who appreciate a courtesy discount once in a while. Yet what do we do? We insult and even embarrass some guests by giving the impression that they are cheapies who are out to beat us out of a buck, or a free meal. *Beat us out of a buck?* Absurd! We made the offer! We even advertised that we wanted both old and new customers to patronize our stores.

Our leases may have five, ten, fifteen, or more years to run. Where is our perspective? We must learn to accept our own coupons with a smile and a thank you, as we give every customer our best quality and service. In effect, our coupon offer worked. We got results. The guest who returns a coupon today can become a repeat customer tomorrow. Refuse to redeem perfectly good coupons, and customers can be lost forever. Couponing has proved to be a most successful marketing tool. But remember that restaurant couponing differs from supermarket merchandising. Be a bit less technical with your guests. Try being more lenient, and watch your personnel breathe a bit more easily as your customers smile and say thank you for giving them every courtesy.

"Hey Mister Can You Spare a Dime?"

One conjures up a scene of a beggar in rags with palm up asking for a handout. It really is rough to be down on one's luck, and have to beg for a handout. It has to be embarrassing to both parties in such a transaction. We never think of things such as this occurring in our establishments. What does this have to do with your foodservice operation? Perhaps nothing. And, maybe a great deal. "Begging" is a hard word. Charity, donations, raffles, tickets, and other forms of do-gooder efforts unquestionably sound better, and are important. The recipients of the dollars and services offered by such charities are the needy and underprivileged. Obviously, we are not speaking out against them. We can only call certain facts and conditions to your attention. You be the judge.

☑ **B/L Recommends:** Guests patronizing your establishment, we believe, should not be subjected to *pressure* to give donations. We have observed service personnel in a variety of operations solicit customers to donate to worthy (and unworthy) causes. Guests cannot always say they "gave at the office" to a charming, personable waitress who may be trying to make her quota. Consequently, guests may end up paying more than they previously planned to spend.

Picture this scenario: The husband not wanting to appear a cheapskate gives a generous donation to the waitress-solicitor. The wife (later on) gives him hell for doing it. He claims it was for a good cause. She reminds him of their own bills. The argument and hard feelings continue. She blurts out, "We are never going back to that restaurant!" He agrees. Who is the loser? You are! Raffle tickets always appear to be a big deal, with the promise of a new car, a trip, or a TV set for the winners. A buck a ticket may not be too much for a try. Some customers do not like to gamble or wish to become involved in certain charitable causes.

Plastic banks placed by organizations and fraternal groups at your cash stand may be a little more subtle. But do not allow such activities to take you or your people away from your main purpose, namely: to serve the best food; to give the best service, so people will want to *return* again and again to your establishment.

Wash Your Hands

With what? We know one manager who refuses to purchase liquid soap for his restroom soap dispensers. He claims people always waste it or break his dispensers. When being inspected, he always claims he just ran out of soap. How poor his judgment. What poor operating procedure.

☑ **B/L Recommends:** Check your operation. Determine if you are exercising poor judgment in cases similar to this. How can you expect your employees and customers to have respect for you if you do not show respect for them and their basic needs? We said customers, too. Unhappy employees will tell their customers that their manager *never* buys soap (meaning he does not care). All the while a "wash your hands" sticker may be prominently displayed over the handsinks.

In many cases employees and customers alike must use the same restrooms. Be aware of how your people are dressed if they are allowed to use your public restrooms. Back of the house personnel often get pretty sweaty, greasy, and dirty. Their appearance may not be too attractive. Do not let your customers get turned off because you neglected to turn on your people to basic cleanliness, neatness, and appearance.

"Sit Someplace Else"

In every establishment, irrespective of size, there are certain counter seats, booths, and tables where management and other personnel seat themselves. These particular seats and tabletops are used for everything from having a cup of coffee to interviewing prospective employees, to resting in between rush periods, gossiping with the help, and talking with sales and service people. You will generally find these seats and tables adjacent to the cash stand, in a rear area, or nearest telephones or kitchen areas. When management, hostesses, and cashiers are not using these "tops" it is not unusual for other crew members to emulate their bosses by sitting there too. Walk into just about any store and you will be able to identify these favorite places by the litter that is invariably left there, such as: newspapers, cups, work papers, schedules, handbags, cigarettes (smoking or crushed) in ashtrays etc. These tops are rarely cleaned and reset with proper silverware and napkin setups. Service personnel usually become accustomed to having these particular "management tables" on their stations. They automatically ignore them. We have known some who refused to reset them, knowing full well they will be messed up again. We have also seen sales representatives automatically take these same seats when asked to wait. Do you recognize the picture? Shouldn't you change this?

☑ *B/L Recommends:* Break the "management table" habit! Sit someplace else if you must sit out front in the guest area of your establishment. Get into the habit of sitting in, and looking at your store, from *every angle*. Notice the dust collecting on the window ledges. Spot the dead flies and cobwebs. Take note of the seats in need of repair. Feel the air-conditioning and heat that may be out of balance. Hear the noises and loud four-letter words that emanate from the kitchen or exhibition area. Listen to the waitresses and waiters gossiping in the service stations when they should be out on the floor. Do not encourage your sales representatives to loiter in your store.

You will keep better control of your complete operation if you use your senses to listen, hear, see, and smell your business from every possible vantage point. You can also be sure that whenever you vacate one of these other tables it will be reset by your personnel and be perfectly ready to receive your guests when they arrive. No more "management table" blues, ugliness, and unprofitable S.O.P. How about it?

I Am Not on Duty

What a familiar phrase. How often have you heard it, or said it? We foodservice people are different from others. Most of us for some reason or another will return to our place of employment when we are off duty. Office workers, plant employees and sales representatives, for example, rarely return to their offices or jobs when they have finished for the day or week. They disappear; they take their full time when they are off. But we, more often than not, take our jobs almost as a way of life. Our friends are often our fellow workers. Most of us like to come back for a cup of coffee, to say hello, to hear how well the store did in sales, to find out if a particular job was completed, and just to gossip. Our restaurants are conveniently open—so, we drop by.

☑ **B/L *Recommends:*** *Develop and enforce a strict policy concerning off-duty personnel.* If you allow them to return, they should be treated as customers. They should not be allowed to enter the rear areas or help themselves to food and drinks. Off-duty employees who are still in uniform should not sit in customer areas. You and they may know they are off, but your guests will not. They will think your people are lazy and inattentive. Be sure there is a guest check for all food and beverages consumed by off-duty people that can be recorded for control purposes. It is your business if certain foods and beverages are to be given free or be discounted. You can pick up the tab and score some points with off-duty employees, if you want to do it. Do not allow some other service person to make up your mind for you by not presenting a check. Let them know that it is a privilege you are extending to them.

Insofar as management is concerned . . . *they are never off duty!* If you, or your assistant, return for any reason whatsoever, you should be prepared to work, help out, give advice, or perform all duties that may be immediately needed. *Management should be presentably attired whenever in the store, and be glad to pitch in.* Your guests and employees recognize you and your salaried staff members. They reason that if you are there, you must be on duty. Those of us who accept the title of "Manager" (or of any other responsible salaried position), must also accept the fact that ours is a 24-hour job. Take your time off, and stay out of your establishment. However, if you do show up, be prepared to help, make a proper appearance, and smile the whole time.

"Close" Counts in This Game Too

Unthinking managers use what we consider to be an expensive way to schedule labor. The night shift schedule reads like this:

5—Close

Obviously, the employees are going to clock in at 5:00 and clock out *whenever* they believe they are finished for the evening. It could be anywhere from one to as much as three hours after the restaurant has closed to customers. Can management afford to leave an open-paycheck decision to those who stand to gain from slow, inefficient closing down procedures each evening?

☑ **B/L Recommends:** No way should you allow your night closing crew to decide *when* to clock out. Never schedule personnel "To Close." *Be specific.* Tell them they will check in at a set hour and that *they must close up and clock out by a specific hour.* You must determine how long they should prep and clean your store after the front door is locked. If your schedule calls for eight hours, and you close at midnight, then your labor chart should read: 5-1:00 a.m. This allows one hour to prep and clean. Anything beyond this is overtime and *must be authorized in advance.* If employees know they cannot fool you, they will get out on time.

Do not accept employee complaints that they cannot finish in one hour (or whatever time you have designated). Return to your store at customer closing time and "help" employees to "see" what to do. Instruct them as to how to do it efficiently. We guarantee you will save many hundreds of dollars a year in so-called "overtime" pay. All you have to do is specifically and intelligently designate the work schedules by precise hours.

The Palace Guard

When you were a youngster did you look through the magazines and travel sections and hope to one day vacation in far-off lands? Magazines and travel posters provided many of us with a pictorial trip abroad to London, Rome, or Athens. And, do you remember the soldiers in their high plumed hats and smart uniforms who marched and stood guard over the priceless possessions and royal persons? What pride. How wonderful we thought it might be to be among the special handpicked people who handled their duties so smartly. Is it too farfetched to compare these guards to our long term employees—those of whom we are so proud, too? We may have excessive turnover with some craft positions, but the majority of us enjoy a permanent cadre of people who have been in our employment for years, or even decades. Agree? Question: *Do we use them properly?* Probably not.

☑ **B/L Recommends:** Your people with years of seniority can be as valuable to you as your customers. Unfortunately, they can also exert a negative influence on your newer personnel. Usually there is no question about their reliability. They always show up on shift. They do their work. But what a pity to see old pros take advantage of their tenure, as they intimidate new managers and fellow employees. With their years of practice and experience, pros should be able to perform perfectly in every situation. So why is it that the majority of them are the first ones to object and refuse to obey our new ideas and sound business principles? People can remain too long. Some just go through the motions as they display false smiles and deliver bored sales presentations. Do they perhaps feel they have earned the right to be cranky, obstinate, and tempermental because they have been there longer than you? We say *no way!* You are the manager, and responsible for your guests, first, last, and always!

It is your job to motivate your old-timers to *guard your house*. You will quickly lose the respect of both the old and new employees if you allow your older ones to bend and break your rules. Those who should set the proper example must do it—or else! On the other hand, you could call your old pros together for a heart-to-heart talk to remind them of their duties and loyalties to you, their restaurant owner, or to their company. Honor their seniority. Give them their pride. Enlist their help. Explain that you cannot afford to accept less than perfection. Expect them to be your leaders and not your antagonists. Plan to meet them half way. Perhaps they are grouchy because they see things which they know to be wrong, that you do not see. Get them to talk. Do not be afraid to say you do not know. Clear the air. There can only be one boss. You had better be that person.

What Have You Done for Me Lately?

Employees believe that their bosses have very short memories. They are convinced that their superiors are too quick to dismiss years of loyal and dedicated service at the first sign of a letdown or mistake. Few claim to be perfect, but owner/managers often expect employees to be absolutely punctual, clean, attentive, industrious, honest—in a word, perfect. Many times bosses fail to take into account that employees have their physical and psychological periods of highs and lows like everybody else. Personnel cannot (and will not) go at full steam at all times. If they do, they will break down, causing owners and guests to suffer the consequences of excessive turnover and poor service.

☑ *B/L Recommends:* Recheck and rewrite your policies with respect to terminations for cause. Insert the words "may be" ahead of the phrase "cause for immediate termination" for some of the lesser offenses. Teach your management team to be more forgiving and understanding *if personnel are deserving of this consideration*. We prefer to strictly enforce terminations for such things as outright disobedience and walking off shift. Other severe, but possibly less damaging infringements may call for short or medium suspension from work, a probation period, or a reprimand. Management can still maintain authority yet keep the respect of the crew when it shows a little compassion.

We have witnessed many incidents wherein employees bent the rules and could have been fired but were not. Managers, in these cases, evaluated whether the offense actually harmed customers and profits. Managers demanded sufficient apologies for the inappropriate actions, thus maintaining morale and discipline, but avoiding the final blow of termination.

Give Your Cooks a Break

One client recently bragged to us that her cooks never take a coffee or lunch break. They just work straight through. Sounds great, doesn't it? We do not agree. You can let them take their breaks and still get your money's worth out of your cooks. Analyze the relationship between yourself and your cooks. A cook is responsible for lining up the galley for the next rush period. He or she must, among the 101 things to do, produce consistent quality and run a clean kitchen. A manager or kitchen supervisor should oversee a cook's work and, at the very least, poke around in the galley to check, touch, taste, and smell all foodstuffs. Cooks like their independence and dislike being checked, but they will respect a boss who knows what is needed. A manager has a responsibility to his or her crew, concept, and customers. When cooks are not prepared there will be drag orders and an out-of-stock condition. Therefore, it becomes necessary that managers properly train their cooks so they will know what to expect in the way of supervision and control.

☑ *B/L Recommends:* Intelligent managers will see to it that their cooks take coffee, smoke, and meal breaks at appropriate times. A manager can break the first cook, and each in turn can break the next person. The manager is then in an excellent position to work one or more stations and freely check everything. Armed with a pencil and notepad he or she can jot down everything that may be needed or that should be cleaned. Cooks returning from their breaks should be met with a list of requirements. Repeat this routine a few times and you should find your list getting smaller and smaller, as your cooks anticipate your wishes. Continue to go into your galley to see and be seen, to assist and inspect. Advantages of being on the right side of the law aside, you will have a well lined up kitchen and a clean and efficient one if you will start off by giving your cooks a break.

Moonlighting

This is the practice of holding a second regular job in addition to one's main job to earn additional income or experience. There are two opposing viewpoints on this subject: ours (management) and theirs (employees). When we were employees it was all right to moonlight. Now that we are in management we are not quite so sure it is so okay for our employees. Agree? Some people cannot handle the physical and psychological drain that serving more than one master can demand. Others cannot cope with the loyalty and dedication required by certain employers. Pulling one shift for one boss then leaving to pull another full or partial shift for some other boss will produce greater earnings for the employee, but possibly less for one or both the employers. And how about the employer-employee relationship?

☑ *B/L Recommends:* You should make it a practice to know exactly who in your employment is working elsewhere. You are paying good wages for a full day's work, and you must insist that everyone deliver their full effort. An employee's "coasting" because he or she is tired from the other job should not be tolerated. Allow people to get away with it and your regular employees will take note and follow suit. Moonlighters often attract a certain respect from their fellow workers. Everyone, with the possible exception of yourself, knows who works elsewhere. Moonlighters are sort of tin heroes. They get around. They see and hear more of what is going on. They have double the opportunity to be exposed to differences in management, gossip, secrets, advertising, promotions, systems, procedures, and pilferage. It is normal to compare. Those who work for more than one employer cannot help but analyze and talk of the advantages and disadvantages they experience. Employees of both crews question these special workers as to what is going on—what jobs are available, the pay rates, and differences in overtime.

Generally, all moonlighters are not necessarily loners, but they do not have one set of loyalties either. Their needs are obvious and very personal: more money! Advancement is not their main objective. Management cannot usually build on these people. They can be disruptive and independent because they have, in a manner of speaking, other income.

Employer-employee relations are based upon *mutual need*. We believe employers should become as important to their employees as is possible. Managers should know if their people are going to make it on what they pay them. Most managers we know prefer to deal with full-time employees than a series of part timers, or moonlighters. When mutual need—the "magical" ingredient—is absent, the relationship will be different. Management must be alert to such subtle differences.

What the Well-Dressed Man Will Wear

Whites, checked pants, aprons, chefs' hats and coats, shoes, and so on may (or should) be required items in your code of apparel. More importantly, do you enforce your dress code? We suggest you do not—not entirely or consistently. Too many houses have allowed their crews to become sloppy, to everyone's disadvantage. You are not a good boss if you allow your personnel to be out of uniform.

☑ *B/L Recommends:* From the bottom up, the Uniform of the Day should be: *Shoes:* Closed, leather, protective-type (no tennis shoes or open sandals). *Pants:* White or checked uniform-type, that fit properly. *Shirt or coat:* White or colored, single or double-breasted, protective, easily laundered. *Scarf:* White or colored, absorbent, decorative with clasp or knot when used to denote status of cook (i.e., one color for line cook, another for management and a third color for cook trainees). *Apron:* Full, folded in half, tied in back or front and fitting completely around the waist for cleanliness, protection, and as a cushion when working against hot and cold surfaces.

We have seen cooks seriously burned because they did not wear aprons. Young cooks frequently believe it is stupid to wear an apron. They like to wear their shirts loose over their pants. This offers no protection whatsoever. Many operators issue two aprons per week to their cooks. Cooks reverse the four sides for maximum wear. The apron string can also hold a side towel so cooks can work clean. *Grooming:* Clean shaven, mustaches trimmed above the lip line, clean fingernails, hair cut above the collar or worn in a net, should be the type of professional appearance required in your house. Professionals who show they are proud of their work and classification can earn the respect of their fellow workers by their neat appearance. *Hat:* Caps, or chef's hats, provide the final touch and are most important for cleanliness and a sharp appearance. We believe amateurs and trainees should *not* be issued a standard hat until they are fully capable of pulling every station. We, in our own restaurants, require trainees to wear the overseas-type bus boy cap until they can properly prepare every dish, clean and work every station, and handle the wheel-order position. Then, and only then, are they awarded a chef's hat (and a pay raise) in recognition of their individual accomplishments. Well-dressed cooks will prepare quality foods. Isn't that what you really want?

Great Way to Lose Employees

How? Lend them money.

☑ *B/L Recommends:* Do not lend money to any employee if you can possibly avoid it. New managers usually learn this lesson the hard way as they fall for sob stories from their people. Certainly you should not make loans to new employees whom you do not yet know or trust. Older employees with many years of experience generally will not ask for loans, as they have learned to live within their incomes. New ones can be dangerous as they "get into you" before they have earned enough money to live on as well as repay money they've borrowed from you. You can be sure that their buddies at work would not lend them the money. So why should you?

Create a policy and stick to it! Allow employees who are short of funds to borrow up to 50 percent of their present paycheck. Be sure they sign an I.O.U. giving you permission to deduct the amount when you give them their pay. Be a nice guy, and 99 times out of 100 you will lose not only your money but the employees to whom you gave the loans.

I Can Get It for You Wholesale

How many of your employees are attracted by an offer to purchase things at less than retail? How often do sales drivers and peddlers stop in your store to trade with your employees, selling them such things as farm-fresh eggs, meats, poultry, clothing, TV's, radios, watches, and other items?

☑ *B/L Recommends:* Stop the practice of allowing suppliers to enter your store to deal independently with your people. The interruptions, cash transactions, personal food purchases can lead to bartering and trades that in all probability will involve *your* merchandise, not to mention your money, and requests for loans that employees may make their great "buys" at so-called "wholesale prices." The wholesalers, the peddlers, and those who may be handling "hot goods" will think you're terrific as they conduct transactions that can only serve to break down internal security and ultimately harm your business.

What a Story Your Tape Can Tell

That cash register of yours is one valuable piece of equipment. It is the heartbeat of your business. It should be handled with great care. Is it possible your personnel are using your register for the wrong things?

☑ *B/L Recommends:* Check your tapes carefully. Count the number of "no-sale" ring-ups (zeroes). One chain we checked had an average of one zero ring-up for every ten transactions. Obviously, more people were going *into* the registers to take something *out* than vice versa. The one acceptable reason for no-cash items is the opening of the register to make change for the convenience of customers. However, it is most unbusinesslike, unprofessional, and asking-for-trouble when managers allow such items to be kept in cash drawers as keys, pens, pencils, paper clips, rubber bands, scratch pads, and other items that have nothing whatever to do with proper cash handling and S.O.P. Reduce to a minimum those reasons why your people should be ringing up "no-sale" transactions on your tapes.

The "Open Door" Policy

Really this procedure should be called, "the open cash drawer heist." A unit manager is asking for big trouble when he or she allows cash handlers or anyone to take and make change with the cash drawer *open* all the time, or in spurts. Isn't it a bit odd that professional cashiers who know the tricks of their trade claim that it is *faster* to take cash using an open drawer? We have frequently proved that those who follow good S.O.P. when handling cash are just as fast and twice as accurate! Quick-cash pros are a whiz at taking guest check after check and making change, all the while totaling up in their heads one or two checks, then removing a corresponding amount from the gross receipts before leaving their shift.

☑ *B/L Recommends:* Allow this practice, and you will rarely balance. You will experience very interesting even-number shortages (plus or minus a few cents which might reflect your normal overages or shortages). In other words, your in-house thief will remove even amounts of currency such as a $5, $10, $20, $50, or $100 bill. You will think someone missed a decimal point and look for an overring wherein a $10.00 sale was inadvertently rung up as $100.00. You may not find it.

Begin today. Enforce a policy that each sale must be rung up and recorded in turn, and that each transaction must be separately completed with the *closing* of the cash drawer.

To press the point: New managers, and especially new franchisees, are most vulnerable to professional cashiers, hosts, and hostesses who really do know what they are doing. New operators are ecstatic at obtaining such people. It becomes one less position about which they have to worry. There is only one problem—pros recognize how naive their new bosses are, and when the need arises (and it always does) they will clip them for a fast buck. As soon as *they know they can get away with it* they will begin to take more serious amounts. *Do not allow an "open drawer" policy!*

Roll Your Own

No, we are not suggesting people once more roll their own cigarettes. However, there are some items that should be rolled before being cashed or counted into your register. Obviously we are referring to the buying of tips from service personnel. It is a good practice. Just do not allow waiters and waitresses to count and exchange *their* loose coin for *your* currency without some sort of control.

☑ *B/L Recommends:* Do buy their coin and singles. Keep on hand a supply of coin wrappers. Instruct service personnel to wrap and initial their wrapped coin before selling it to your cash register. Always insist that someone else check the exchange. It is good business on your part to know approximately how well your people are doing in the area of tips. Buying change and singles will give you a fair idea. Just do not let your employees get the idea they can go into your register on their own. You may be the one who gets "rolled."

Opening Banks: Snares and Cures

Most operations use some sort of an opening fund to fuel the cash register at the start of each business day. The amount of money in the fund was probably decreed by someone back in the early days of the store's history. The place where the opening bank is stashed was probably designated at the same time. An ingrained, set routine is the result. The person charged with opening the front end pulls the bank from its hideaway and fills the cash drawer. The day is then off to a very shaky start. *The bank was not counted*. In the hours following, several boo-boos will occur as guest checks are rung up. Starting out with a cash error complicates accounting procedures. Ultimately, someone has to decide if the cash that cannot be located should be made up from their own personal funds. It is either that or listen to the guy in charge scream about goof-ups. Both choices are very unpalatable from an employee's standpoint. Frequently it leads to an attempt, conscious or not, to create a daily cash overage as a matter of self-protection.

☑ *B/L Recommends:* Cash handling miscues have to be minimized, not compounded by superficial management direction. Mere insistence that everything balance out when it is time to make the daily deposit ultimately brings on other problems. *The opening bank does not have to be a sacred, fixed amount of money.* A variable bank forces a cash count at closing and opening. Be fair to your people and yourself. Talk to the night closing crew to determine if they have been using their own money to even out the numbers. A good cash handling S.O.P. requires that money and tape balance out at the close of each shift.

Park It Someplace Else!

Sure, your status as a manager or owner should entitle you to a special parking spot at your store. But is that parking place worth what it can cost? One manager got the point after he evicted some troublesome youngsters. The only slashed tires in the parking lot that night were on the car parked in the slot reading "Reserved for Manager." Even if there is no sign, parking in one selected spot is a bad habit.

☑ *B/L Recommends:* Friends, ex-employees, suppliers and anyone who just wants to fool around (with your business) will spot your habits if you consistently use one set parking place. *When a habit-trapped manager's parking slot is empty, it is an advertisement for trouble*. We have on occasion proven this point to operators by asking them to park their cars as much as a block away and walk to work. This gambit has turned up everything from a variety of guests enjoying free meals in the front end on down to food packages being retailed out the back door to trash collectors. Being unpredictable is not the same as being sneaky. It is a practical method to keep the staff on their toes and a trifle more than normally honest.

What's Your Area of Competence?

The effectiveness of a restaurant manager can be judged by many standards. One way is the length of the office telephone cord. If it is a six-foot cord and the manager is usually hooked to the phone during the rush period, then he has about a *six-foot area of competence*. The theory being that if anything goes wrong inside the length of the cord, the manager will quite likely notice it and take some sort of corrective action. Naturally, this is not always the case. A lesser area of competence is scored when a manager elects to do paperwork or interview sales representatives at his other desk during rush periods. Since few restaurant desks are six feet long, this rates about a four on the competence scale. *Score 100 for the manager that is with the crew and guests during rush periods*.

☑ *B/L Recommends: Nothing should be allowed to interfere with guest service during rush periods*. These are the few hours of each day when a restaurant has an opportunity to turn a profit. The profit depends on how well everything is coordinated. That's the primary duty of a manager. With a firm policy of *no phone calls,* interviews or paperwork during peak business times, a manager's competency score will go up right along with store profits.

Your Best Friends Won't Tell You

Do you look your very best in your store? We are suggesting that perhaps you have a few personal traits which, if they were changed, would really enhance your position with those with whom you work.

☑ **B/L Recommends:** Do the "mirror, mirror on the wall" bit. Ask yourself if you need the scraggly beard, long sideburns, untrimmed mustache, bushy eyebrows, hairy ears, extra long or dirty fingernails, the open shirts, the pants that are too tight or too short, and any other characteristics that might turn off people. You are every bit as much on stage as your service personnel. Managers must set the example. A double standard is never good. Take a fresh look at yourself, then answer this question: Would you patronize a place where the manager looks the way you do? You are the greatest asset to your store, but only if you look sharp, set the proper example, and show everyone by your actions and appearance that they are in good hands with you.

We Swear—It's Not Good

Many of us speak two languages: English and Profanity. Perhaps we do not use the King's English properly, but at least we try. However, those of us who use four-letter words, gutter or back-room talk can cause a great deal of trouble and misunderstanding with our employees and guests. It's not funny to be seated in a dining room and hear a lot of swear words coming out of the kitchen.

I remember how I rushed back to my dish section one evening to determine why there was a holdup with supplies. In my anxiousness, I said "Goddamn it—let's get these dishes out front." My dishwasher glared at me, removed his apron, and said "I don't work for people who use the Lord's name in vain." I washed dishes for the rest of the night. He was right. I was wrong. I had caused turnover, unnecessarily, because I thoughtlessly used profanity. Most service personnel do not like to cope with management's emotional ups and downs. They cannot get a good psychological reading on *how to handle us*, or how to react, especially when management is inconsistent—happy one moment, mad and swearing the next.

☑ **B/L Recommends:** *Think before you talk*. Keep your cool. Do not be so unpredictable as to run hot and cold on your employees. Frankly, most cannot take it for long. They will quit—not because they were reprimanded for their errors—but because of the manner in which they were embarrassed and bawled out. Do you like to be sworn at? Put yourself in their position. You are not tougher because you swear. Try holding your voice and your emotions down, and keep four-letter words to a minimum. It cuts the employee panic factor.

Dates to Remember

When it was finally completed, the company's first operations manual was a joy to behold. It had systems and instructions that were the fruit of years of testing and hard work. The manuals cost about $300 a copy to produce. Naturally, the company was concerned about security, so each of the 70 store managers was required to sign a receipt when taking custody of a manual. In less than four months, from an operation standpoint, the company was in far worse shape than before it issued the manual. Some managers had manuals, others did not. Chaos got inserted into the chain of command. *In order to quash the rampant confusion, all manuals had to be recalled.* It was then necessary to print additional manuals before chainwide redistribution could be accomplished. It was a costly, time-consuming lesson in administration.

☑ **B/L Recommends:** *Think through every administrative action.* Routine memos, directives, and receipts can create confusion and expense unless they are carefully executed and reach all concerned parties. In the above example, the receipts signed by the managers did not carry a dateline. Instructions were unclear as to whether the manual was to accompany the manager when he was transferred, or stay at the store. There were a lot of transfers. The payroll department had verbal orders to recover the manuals when a manager was separated from the company. This was overlooked when the secretary who processed separations was transferred to data processing. In the preparation of any company communication, the first item to put on paper is the date. That way, when the confusion sets in you at least have an idea when it all started.

GUIDELINES
FOR MANAGEMENT

What you learn
after you know it all
is what really counts.

9

GUIDELINES FOR MANAGEMENT

The words we use in speaking to superiors and subordinates can often be misunderstood. We do not say things the way we mean them to be heard and understood. We are in too much of a hurry to think before we speak.

Perhaps you will recognize this scene: the company president casually asks Joe, the supervisor, if he has seen Harry, the vice-president. Joe sees Harry a bit later and misinterprets the question, telling Harry, "You had better get over to see the boss real quick; he's looking for you!" Harry drops what he's doing, finds the boss, and asks, "You wanted me?" The president answers, "No, I only wanted to know if you were in the building." It matters little who was at fault. The communicator did not get the correct message to the "communicatee."

Guidelines for management are just that: helpful hints how we are perceived and misunderstood, and what we can do about our styles of using authority, which may often serve to push away the very people who can make us great.

Here is your first lesson—a short course in human relations:

The 6 most important words	*I admit I made a mistake*
The 5 most important words	*You did a good job*
The 4 most important words	*What is your opinion?*
The 3 most important words	*If you please*
The 2 most important words	*Thank you*
The most important word	*We*
The least important word	*I*

Managing the Manager's Hours

Part of the science of restaurant management is getting things to happen within appropriate time frames. Outside of rising and falling demand for meals, everything happening in a store is keyed to the manager's actions. Therefore if a store is to achieve maximum productivity, the manager's hours on the job have to be carefully plotted.

Generally, unit managers are told quite explicitly what they are expected to accomplish. Unfortunately, the equally important topic of *when and how to get things done* is frequently ignored. This puts managers in the difficult position of having to *react* to situations already in some form of deterioration. Initiative is lost; costly inefficiency is the result.

Some unit managers simply ignore certain things that need attention. An alarmingly large group seeks a less demanding career in other areas of industry. But other unit managers attempt to solve their problems by putting in extra hours on the job. Naturally, it is the hard workers who earn promotions. Yesterday's unit managers are today's supervisors. In effect, inefficiency becomes self-perpetuating.

Managing a restaurant is a complex business, and demands a high degree of personal organization. Long hours on shift are a poor substitute. The hour-to-hour schedule below was prepared as part of a management improvement program for a coffee shop chain. It was designed to show managers where they should be in their various activities throughout the day. It was not intended to be used as an inflexible timetable. Supervisors for this chain reported a marked increase in efficiency for all units, once managers became accustomed to the routine.

Some of the items listed may not be germane to your operation. However, this schedule can be easily revised or adjusted as required.

Manager's Schedule
(Post over office desk)

8 a.m. to 9 a.m.
Arrival: Inspect restaurant parking lot and front of building as you walk toward entrance. Check amount of change in register. Speak to each employee on shift. Verify backup in the kitchen. Did all crew members check in on time? Has anyone called in sick? Take immediate steps to bring crew up to strength. Check correctness of deliveries.

9 a.m. to 10 a.m.
Receive deliveries. Inspect for completion of work assignments made yesterday. Inspect for evidence of good cleanup by closing crew. Inventory all

storage areas and prepare to place orders. Place orders with authorized low bidders. Inspect kitchen readiness. Inspect bus station readiness. Have supplies and food products delivered to kitchen and bus stations so that all is ready for lunch.

10 a.m. to 11 a.m.
Open safe and count all drops from preceding day. Prepare bank deposit. Complete required paperwork related to previous day's business. Check all time cards and enter hours worked for all employees who worked yesterday. Go to the bank to deposit receipts and buy coin and small bills. Upon return from bank, sell required amount of coin or small bills to the cash register.

11 a.m. to 12 noon
Go into kitchen and give cook a break. While spelling the cook, inspect area for cleanliness and status of supplies. When cook returns, give him or her list of deficiencies to correct before lunch starts. Break cashier, host or hostess, start working floor as lunch starts to build. Verify correctness of the station assignments for serving personnel. Verify coverage by service assistants. When cashier returns, make final inspection of both front and back of house.

12 noon to 1 p.m.
Work the floor through lunch, if possible. When necessary, go into the kitchen to help cook for short periods. Work the front of the pass bar. Inspect plates for completeness and neatness of presentation. Assist the serving personnel in assembling orders and speeding service. Be available to customers with questions or complaints. Take cash, seat parties, make sure the waiting line is moving smoothly, pour coffee: be the manager.

1 p.m. to 2 p.m.
Continue working the floor, supervising the pass bar, and when necessary, helping in kitchen. As lunch tapers off, do not do for people what they can do themselves. Supervise the cashier as she or he closes stations and breaks serving personnel. Supervise the start of cleanup in the kitchen. Supervise the cleanup of the dishwashing area. Make sure the kitchen is re-stocked. Supervise the start of prep work for supper. Order lunch and eat.

2 p.m. to 3 p.m.
If this is going to be a late night, clear out of the restaurant and come back ready to do a good job. If it is a normal day, spend *no less* than 30 minutes formulating a plan to take care of problems you know will come up tomorrow. Take your heavy paperwork and scheduling plans to a table in the middle of the dining room. When you hide in your office, you are not in the restaurant.

Take a table where you can see the front door, the kitchen, your cashstand, and customers. Listen to what is happening in the store. Let your customers see that you are an administrator, too. Speak to customers as they arrive. Get up and solve problems, if necessary. Interview job applicants, if there are any.

3 p.m. to 4 p.m.
Gear up for shift changes. Have day shift personnel completed their work, or are they leaving part of it for the night shift? Are there any people calling in sick? Must scheduled personnel be replaced? Do it now. Is supper prep work completed? Are kitchen and bus stations stocked? Have major cleanup projects scheduled for this quiet period been completed? Prepare list of items to be accomplished during the night shift.

4 p.m. to 5 p.m.
Night manager arrives. Together you tour the restaurant. You cover all potential problem areas. Give night manager list of things to be done. Communicate with each other.

5 p.m. to 6 p.m.
Night manager assumes responsibility for restaurant. Complete final paperwork, final scheduling. Lock up storage areas, as called for in the standard operating procedure. Make final check with night manager. Go home.

Intensive Care Program

Have you ever stopped to consider that your business may be in the throes of a heart attack? Your cash flow may have hardening of the arteries. There may not be enough new blood or new ideas getting into your mainstream of activity. Your color is beginning to pale. Your business does not look too good. It may not have long to live. Can you call in a doctor for a cure? Who can you turn to for help?

☑ *B/L Recommends:* If you cannot get someone to make a house call, then we suggest you take your own pulse; make your own prognosis and plan to place your business into an immediate *intensive care program*. Plan your treatment carefully. Set aside a week, two weeks, a month—preferably a period that closely coincides with your accounting period. Pull out all the stops! Conduct an employee meeting, or at the very least a management meeting. Clue in everyone as to what you are up to.

Do one or several of the following things: Place your operation on C.O.D. Do not buy or pay for any products or services that are not absolutely necessary. Re-schedule your help. Rewrite and squeeze your labor schedules to save as many half hours and full hours as you can. Count your monies often to make sure they tally with your daily cash register readings as closely as possible. Check your guest checks and order sheets just as carefully to be sure everything has been prepared against some sort of an order form. Pull a beginning and ending inventory covering the period you have selected. Write up a dozen do's and don'ts if you do not already have some employee policies. Post them. Have each employee initial them. Advise them that they will be strictly enforced.

Put in as many hours on-shift as you can. Get close to your people. Work with them. Show that you can get involved. Definitely open and/or close your operation when you can. Try to have someone you can trust in your store at all times when you cannot be there. Touch your foods and beverages. Work your salaried people overtime. Allow no one to work over-schedule (collect extra time and pay) without your express permission. Eliminate the night maintenance people if you can. Keep everything locked. Force your crew to come to you or your assistants for all keys. Teach them to make fewer trips to your storerooms, and to make each trip a payload. Check your garbage cans. Stop all possible leaks and areas of loss. Put out new or clean menus. "Clean up the joint!" Concentrate on customer areas and services. Analyze your results.

Remember, you are the doctor and patient all wrapped up into one. What you prescribe may save your business life. The patient is critically ill. It might die unless you apply every possible diagnosis and treatment. And your post-operative treatment will be just as important as the *intensive care program*. Your follow through is vital to your health.

How Are Your Ratios Doing These Days?

Ever count those extra unnecessary trips that you and your dining room service personnel have to make because there weren't sufficient chinaware, silverware, and glassware in their proper places to be used? Ever notice how often your customers receive their food dished up on platters when it should have been placed on plates; soup served in coffee cups instead of soup cups, and so forth? Really, it's no joke!

☑ *B/L Recommends:* Know your seating capacity, customers, and turnover per rush period, and the frequency of use of each item of serviceware you need to properly sell each food and beverage item on your menu. This suggestion equally applies to fast food operations that use paper goods and plastic items. Compute your needs based upon your storeroom capacity, dining room or counter storage areas, kitchen inventories, dish section capacity, and labor factors for the complete recycling of all items once they have been used. You might use this rule-of-thumb idea as a starting point in your operation. For example: coffee cups, saucers, and spoons are generally the most popular pieces of serviceware. Maintain a ratio to your seating capacity of at least three to one. If a house seats 100, it should have on hand a minimum of 300 cups, 300 saucers, and 300 spoons. This allows for one full set on each table for each seat, one set in the kitchen or service station, and one set in reserve or in the dish section. On the other hand, for example, your needs might only require a ratio of one-half to one on such seldom used items as soup bowls or a unique fish dish that you might only use a dozen times during each rush period. A proper ratio of all items will also reduce "dishwasher fatigue." Your valuable serviceware will last longer and so will your personnel, who will no longer have to apologize to your customers as they force them to eat or drink from oddball items because you, the owner or manager, did not maintain a stock ratio adequate to your seating capacity needs.

"There Will Be a 45-Minute Wait"

Certainly this is a pleasant enough phrase. We all have heard similar statements from hosts and hostesses. Even if you have a reservation, you still look at your party with helplessness and inquire if everyone wants to wait or leave. You are about to begin what should be a lovely eating experience with a *negative* factor, a long wait—one you had not anticipated. You look around. You see several open tables. You notice the place is busy, but not *that* busy. You assume the person working the door knows how fast the turnover will be. You hate to keep asking "how long?" You still are not sure whether to stay. You had not planned on this delay. You timidly ask again. The reply comes swiftly, "Your name isn't up yet—it will still be a good half-hour!" Your party decides to leave. Had you stayed five minutes longer you would have been seated.

☑ *B/L Recommends:* Owners and operators of establishments that will on occasion or frequently have a waiting line must know the turnover time of their dining rooms. We believe we can trust most owners and managers because they know the value of keeping guests happy. They can be counted on to see that everyone is seated in the shortest possible time. However, it is too often a different story with your hired help who work the door. We have observed houses where instruction was somehow left that when a given number of pages had been filled with the names of guests, the wait time will automatically be one hour. In our opinion, this is ridiculous. Many factors can affect customer turnover, such as open tables; tables that have not yet been "pulled"; a lack of supplies; problems in the kitchen; slow food; slower service; size of parties; number of courses to be served, and so forth. Similarly, there are just as many factors that will have a positive effect on turnover. Guests may have some nearby attraction to visit; everything may be working just perfectly from the back of the house to the cashstand. Your turnover time may unaccountably be shorter than usual.

We recently became involved in such a situation. Our party of four was told by a young hostess at an ocean-front dinner house that our wait would be 45 minutes. We could see names on the list (mostly two's and four's), customers waiting in the lounge, the help moving well in the dining room, and, quite a few open tables. The hostess on this busy Sunday evening did not understand her duties and responsibilities. We knew we would not have to wait any 45-minutes. We waited 25 *minutes*. During our wait we counted exactly 16 people who refused to remain for the ficticious 45-minute wait that had now somehow grown to *one hour!*

Floor personnel must be taught to understand their turnover flow. Guess-work will usually be incorrect. Instruct your people to mark the time opposite every few names to learn just how fast they are being seated. The main thing is to avoid a stock answer. We always recommend an unusual comment such as: "Your wait will be only 13 minutes, or 37 minutes, or one hour and four minutes." Said with a smile and with the knowledge that you will be fairly accurate, your guests will also smile as they check their watches to check you. The introduction of a bit of fun, personality, and accuracy will keep many a customer from leaving or becoming unhappy in your house.

Go to Blazers!

Isn't your operation unique? Haven't you worked hard to develop special foods and services? Don't you take great pride in what your name and establishment stand for? Do business people and neighbors in your community stop you on the street to smile and say hello?

☑ *B/L Recommends:* Become a show-off! Show how proud you are of yourself, your concept, your management team, corporate personnel, and employees. Develop a blazer patch with your name and design embroidered onto it. Attach it to any color blazer coat, or purchase blazer jackets of one color and style for all your key personnel. Everyone will think better of you. Your personnel will take more pride in working for your company. Customers will appreciate seeing someone in management "working the floor" who really belongs. Bankers and local V.I.P.'s will relate better to you. You will have that look of success. You and your people will be the talk of your town wherever and whenever you show up in your company's colors and blazers.

Are You Operating a Restaurant, Supermarket, or Candy Store?

By the look of some cashstands, counters, and entry ways, customers may have trouble determining whether they are in a restaurant or a combination drugstore and supermarket. Have you checked your cashstand lately? Some-how your little five-cent mint displays have grown to include the damndest array of candies, bars, aspirins, cough drops, gums, cigars, cigarettes, etc. And how about those very nice expensive custom-printed solid chocolate bars that you believe help you to advertise your place of business?

☑ *B/L Recommends:* There is a good chance you are not selling as many of these extras as you may think. The rip-off by both your customers and employees can be enormous over a period of but a few months. Rack jobbers and candy wholesalers tell you how much you "sold," as they regularly build up your inventory, tell you the latest joke, and get you to sign for the merchandise you have purchased. Your store may well be one of the best stops on their routes. The challenge in being in this type of retail business is to *sell* the merchandise before you lose it. Customers, employees, and maintenance people know this merchandise is rarely inventoried. And anyway, you can afford a twenty-cent candy bar or roll of mints, can't you?

We question whether you are really receiving a good return on your time and investment from your "sweet shoppe." Return to your basic concept. Just what is your real business? Do not try to be all things to all people.

Quality and Service Are Worth Waiting For

You make a date. You arrive at a nice restaurant. You may wait. You are seated. Menus are presented. Mouth-watering descriptions entice you to order. You are about to, but are stopped by a *message* that reads, "Allow 30-40 minutes for preparation." You hesitate. You order something else. You wish you had not changed your mind.

We can appreciate the need for this sort of a warning, but in only the most unusual of operations and with only the most unique of chef's creations. Why this warning in a local lunch, dinner, and take-out restaurant where reasonably fast turnover is desired? We closely observed one such operation. We questioned several waitresses and cooks who explained that the items really did not take that long to be prepared and served. Many customers were, however, talked out of ordering some of the items. So again, why the warning?

☑ **B/L Recommends:** Feature items on your menu you are proud to serve. Quality must be your first consideration. If they are worthy of your culinary efforts they are most assuredly worthy of your customers' patience and ultimate enjoyment. Do not feature such time-consuming specialties if yours is a fast-turn house. Depending upon the spot, it is not unusual for guests to place their orders, enjoy their round of drinks, take wine, appetizers, soup, and/or salad before consuming their entrees. If the food is coming out of the kitchen properly, and the service personnel are alert, the specialty of the house can usually be served without too much delay. Again, *do not hinder* the sale of items you want to push either for the higher gross sales or word-of-mouth recommendations you can receive from such special creations.

If your atmosphere, interior decor, and service are conducive to a pleasant eating experience, we guarantee your guests will be unaware of a so-called 30-minute wait, especially when the wait holds the promise of a great dish. Be more concerned with the quality of your foods than you are with the clock. *Quality* is worth waiting for.

Country Club Blues and Bright Spots

Banquets can be beautiful. Special occasions can be delightful. One of the nicest places to hold or attend such affairs is a local country club. The vast panorama of greens and fairways, the tennis courts, swimming pools, and the members who look so very athletic in their colorful outfits make a great scene. Parties, sit-down or buffet dinners scheduled for dozens to hundreds of club members can also be a real headache. Big events are expected to be grand. Members and their guests can be most demanding. The best of plans can go wrong, which can spell big losses for the foodservice operator. For example, what do you do when you have a full reservation list, your crew is on hand, your food has been prepared, and it *rains?* The golfers and tennis players who usually hit the 19th hole for a drink or two before they shower and/or dress for dinner *do not show up.* . . .

☑ **B/L Recommends:** Every house that operates on a fixed dinner program and guest list of arrivals must protect itself whenever possible. A "reservation only" policy is for everyone's protection. Accept reservations, but be sure to obtain every possible phone number contact and guest name that you can. Sudden rains and thunder showers can throw cold water on everybody's plans and cause members to become no-shows. You must make a quick decision— serve dinner, or close for the evening? Experience has shown that only a mere handful of guests will show. Use your telephone. Reach every possible guest on your reservation list. Cancel the evening. Store your foods, and send your service personnel home.

On the brighter side, country club chefs and managers, in our opinion, do not take full advantage of all the excellent public relations opportunities available to them. They should take the time to *write a regular column* for their club newspaper or bulletin. Eating and drinking are among the most important aspects of all clubs who have such facilities. There are any number of subjects to be written about, such as new personnel; specialties of the house; names, occasions, and dates of parties served, etc. Remember to use names. Club members like to see their names in print. At least they will be able to read their names in your "Dining Room Column" even if they cannot win any club tournaments.

Chefs Are Beautiful People—But Where Are They?

Chefs, or cooks if you prefer, come in all colors and sizes. They speak many languages, but all do their real talking with their hands, senses, and hearts. Their products are the foods we eat. Their creativity, and the respect with which they handle foodstuffs speak of the quality of their training and experience. The old clichés no longer apply. Today's chefs are not always throwing temper tantrums. They ask for and demand quality, taste, appearance, and cleanliness. Is that wrong? Cooks are some of the hardest working, proudest people in our society. Yet where are they? They are busy in their kitchens. Most chefs virtually run the whole show. Many receive the credit they deserve. Many are neglected and ignored. Fortunately, proud professionals will not allow themselves to do a poor job. A chef's work is never done. Strong legs are merely the first things cooks must have. They are the very backbone of our restaurants. Owners, managers, and salespeople see them. But, how about our guests? Shouldn't they, too, have an opportunity to see these V. I. P.'s (very important persons) of our kitchens?

☑ **B/L Recommends:** *Show off your chefs and cooks.* We happen to believe one of the most unique and universally recognized uniforms in the world is a chef's outfit. The tall, starched and pleated chef's hat squared over the eyebrows, the smart scarf with a unique knot or ring, the fresh all white chef's coat, double-breasted and buttoned hanging down over all white or checked pants, the folded apron tied about the waist with the side towel over the apron string, and the black shoes all together leave no doubt as the occupation of these special people. We remember the time it took to earn the privilege to wear a chef's hat. It signified we knew what we were doing. It did not automatically come with our first time card as it does today in all too many shops. We were proud to be accepted by our peers. Once christened a chef, we dared not produce poor quality. We learned to work fast and clean. We liked to walk out into our dining rooms to see and be seen, to talk to our guests.

It was more than showing off. Guests like to see their chef. His or her presence on the floor says a great deal. It shows the cook cares. Who would believe this smart-appearing person would dare to serve TV dinners or dish up just any old food? No way. One look, one handshake, a short conversation, a smile from the chef is all the reassurance a guest needs to know his or her food has been properly prepared to order.

The $10,000 Cover Up

"White tablecloth" restaurants have always paid the price for quality laundry and linens. The extra touch of class has proved to be worth the total investment. Freshly cleaned and starched tablecloths with matching napkins and other accessories help to make even an ordinary meal a finer eating experience. However, things that are white in color are always difficult to keep clean and fresh in appearance. Managers know that almost any dish, glass, or condiment can leave a mark on a white cloth, compelling employees to turn the covers more frequently, use placemats, or have them cleaned before being put to further use. The trouble, of course, is that managers have never had to pay so much to rent, purchase, and maintain their table covers as they do now. You can save a laundry bag full of money.

☑ **B/L Recommends:** Switch to colored and patterned tablecloths and napkins. Patterned tablecloths will last longer and look better than white cloths. Cigarette burns, repairs, dirt spots, and smudges can hardly be noticed except perhaps under the brightest of lights and scrutiny. The executive chef who told us of his success with this idea figures he has saved in excess of $10,000 a year in this single area of his table service. Can't you *pattern* your operation after his suggestion?

Promises, Promises, Promises

Do you remember the character traits you used to value most when you were a kid? Is it possible that the trait you felt to be most important had to do with your friends keeping their promises to you? How disappointed were you when people forgot you, or forgot to do something you felt to be important, for which they had crossed their hearts and hoped to die. You were vulnerable and could be hurt quite easily. But as you matured, you learned to place a bit less faith in people. Cynically, you now even expect people to break their promises. And now that you are in business, is it possible that you may be the one who is breaking the promises? Your guests can be easily hurt when they receive less in quality and service than what they were told or led to expect.

☑ *B/L Recommends:* Identify those promises that you really want to make and keep. Literally *read your menu to your crew.* It is not as ridiculous as it sounds. Your menu is a list of promises of the foods, services, qualities, and prices that you wish to give. Your menu is so commonplace to you and your personnel that everyone almost ignores it. We suggest that many operators, and their cooks and service personnel have never really concentrated on what each item and its descriptive phrase means. For instance, "prepared to order" does not mean serving up sandbagged meats that have been pre-cooked on one side so that cooks can more quickly prepare and serve a hamburger sandwich. "Prepared to order" means that the meat does not go down until the order has been placed. "Homemade" soups, chili, and stews are not supposed to come out of #10 cans. "Sliced tomatoes on crisp lettuce" does not mean soft, spoiled, watery, half-smashed slices on a wilted, warm piece of lettuce.

Speed may be important to your operation, but sandbagging and other shoemaker tricks can ruin the taste or appearance of your foods. Many of our cooks in a true sense are *not cooks at all;* they are production people. They often lack a sensitivity to what they are doing. They allow foods to deteriorate, burn, soak, dry out, wrinkle, and otherwise become unattractive. Adjectives such as fresh, wholesome, nutritious, hot, zesty, crisp, ice-cold, and fluffy promise good eating. Your crew will only care if you do. Promise what you will—only, *keep the promises you make.*

I Scared Me-Self

Red Skelton, a most beloved comedian, used to perform in a radio skit about a little boy who usually got himself into a peck of trouble. Often he would make loud noises then cry, "I scared meself."

Managers often frighten employees with loud voices and reprimands. They do not mean to panic their people—they just do. We know one owner who literally shouts every sentence. He uses his hands as if he were a sailor sending semaphore signals. To watch and listen to him as he deals with his employees is to see that everyone must be in a constant state of panic. He can frighten the faint-of-heart even with a compliment.

☑ *B/L Recommends:* Cool it! Keep your voice and mannerisms under control. *Do not panic your people or customers.* You are their leader. Personnel will follow your lead. If you yell, they will yell. Remember, eating is an emotional experience; it should be done in a calm, comfortable atmosphere. It is not unusual for employees and guests to leave feeling psychologically drained by the strain of a panicky situation. People cannot give their best performance when they are nervous and on edge. Everyone knows you are the boss. You do not have to yell, or put on a big dramatic show to prove it.

Menu Overkill

Many *fast food* operations are being turned into *slow food losers* by ill-advised menu additions. There is a real danger in trying to be all things to all customers. A big menu variety may appear impressive, but actually it complicates things for your staff, and serves to confuse guests. Further, it can harm the image a store has for one or more good specialty dishes.

Too often we think our competitors have the right ideas and our own stores do not. Franchisees and operators of limited menu houses generally succumb to the pressures to serve something else in addition to their mainstay. Hamburger shops add chicken, and vice versa. Fish 'n' chippers pick up sandwiches and soups. As more items go on the menu, identity gets blurred and food costs escalate. Operations with limited equipment and cooking capability can only hope to produce acceptable quality so long as things are kept simple.

☑ *B/L Recommends: Do not give in to the temptation to be all things to all people.* Recognize your assets, liabilities, and potential. It is far better to do one or a few things really well than to do many things just adequately.

Mending Menu Leaks

Sometimes it is difficult to identify menu problems. Take the case of a young enterprise that featured a do-it-yourself salad bar. The volume was thriving, but the net was not up to expectations. The featured items were a $1.69 salad plate and a 99¢ salad bowl. Both were excellent values. However, a guest check audit revealed that the bowls were outselling plates five to one. Repricing or eliminating the bowls would risk the ire of too many customers. *The solution was to move the bowl from the a la carte section to the combination side of the menu.* It was offered in conjunction with an array of sandwiches. A little staff retraining and suggestive selling instruction started profits on the climb.

☑ *B/L Recommends: When volume and profits do not match up the way they should, you may have a price trap in your menu.* A guest check audit will usually pinpoint the problem. Drastic menu alterations are seldom called for; all it takes is a little creative readjustment.

Scrambled Egos: A Costly Item on the Menu

Of all the pastimes available to executives in the restaurant industry, one of the most dangerous is menu tinkering. It is perfectly logical to assume no menu is perfect and any menu can be improved. But translating thought to deed is where companies run into expensive problems.

We recently unraveled a situation where menu tinkering almost led to the collapse of an otherwise excellent chain operation. The company had a new director of operations for its 14 full service units. He felt he needed a new, fancy hamburger platter on the menu. He wanted to add some class and profits to what he considered a dull list of menu items. *His thinking did not coincide with that of the company's executive chef.*

The director of operations went over the chef's head and won approval for his project. The chef elected not to make an issue of the matter. He just buried the new platter in a list of burger items appearing on the customer menu. The meal offered highly popular items like sautéed mushrooms, bleu cheese dressing, a fresh chopped green salad, and fries. The menu description read like a sales pitch for a barbed-wire band aid.

The director of operations soon learned customers were not ordering the platter. He countered the chef's maneuver by instructing cooks to make the dish an outstanding buy. Load on the french fries, he ordered. The fries got sopped in the bleu cheese topping. The executive chef issued a memo regarding the hazards of over-portioning. The director of operations told the supervisor of serving personnel to have the waitresses do some suggestive selling. *She rejected this vulgar proposal.* Like the executive chef, she resented interference in her domain.

From that point on, more company projects got iced than a fish market's inventory.

Store managers became confused and frustrated trying to placate the warring factions at company headquarters. Morale slumped along with company standards for quality and service.

Because of the personal stakes involved, a clash between the middle-level executives was probably inevitable. Unfortunately, the battleground they selected was the company's most valuable piece of property, its menu. The war damages to business and to individual careers were appalling.

☑ **B/L Recommends:** *Establish rigid criteria for menu alterations.* All plans should be set forth in writing. The format should be concise. In four paragraphs, the originator should cover (1) objective; (2) method; (3) projected costs & profits; (4) system for evaluation. Research or back-up data should appear as addendum to the basic letter. The letter should be sent to all department heads for comment. Comments must appear in writing. Either the plan is disapproved at this point, or the letter and consolidated comments are used to establish the operational directive. The directive states what is required from each department and the deadlines for completion. The operations directive is actually a game plan that emphasizes teamwork and cooperation. It is less costly to complete paperwork in advance on a menu change than attempt to salvage customers, workers, and a company treasury damaged by interior conflicts. *A restaurant's menu is a fragile item.* It must be protected from executive egos, and tinkering by shareholders and company do-gooders.

Go on a Diet with Food Advice

It is nice to be regarded as an expert on food by friends and associates. It is not nice to be sued for imparting advice that falls in the realm of medical practice. *You can be seen as trying to play doctor* if you recommend certain foods or combinations as being healthier or less fattening. The same applies if you prescribe vitamins and calorie control nostrums. Legalistically, we are living in troubled times.

☑ *B/L Recommends: Be careful.* Don't expose yourself to a lawsuit while trying to be helpful to an overweight customer. Stick to home-style cooking. Forget home cures and avoid lawsuits.

The Tip Envelope

The splitting of tips by waiters and waitresses with others is often an embarrassing non-verbal exchange. Buspersons stand around and wait for someone to hand over their tip money. *Waitresses and waiters provide the handout without enthusiasm, or even constructive criticism.* Those who receive splits always believe they have it coming to them automatically. On the other hand, serving personnel giving the money often wish to complain that they did not receive all the help they believe they should have. To avoid trouble, they simply say nothing and just give a smaller split. Soon the buspersons quit and the whole routine begins to repeat itself.

☑ *B/L Recommends:* Communication is the key to keeping everyone happy. We believe waiters and waitresses should not just complain to managers when they feel they are getting poor support service. *They should tell buspersons, cooks, or whoever, exactly how they feel about the quality of the work supplied.* This can be accomplished through the adoption of small tip envelopes for the use of waiters and waitresses. The size of the envelope is 4¼ x 2½", the cost is about two cents, plus imprint charges. They can be printed with a space for the name of the recipient, date, comments on service supplied, and a signature line for the use of the donor.

Maintain a stock of the envelopes at the cashstand for waiters and waitresses to use when they hand out tip money to other members of the staff. That way, *their compliments and complaints go directly to the source.* The system encourages greater cooperation and eliminates misunderstandings. You will find, as our clients have, that the compliments far outnumber the complaints checked on the envelopes.

```
TIPS for _____Date_____

The quality, speed, and overall support you gave
me was:

_____Excellent (my guests were happy)
_____Above average
_____Good
_____Needs improvement (see other side)

     Thank you_____
```
flap

Training Begins at Home

There is a lot of discussion these days about employee training. *Nobody talks about a training program for guests.* Friends of the management, investors, relatives, and all their children enjoy a special status in the restaurant world. They are the V.I.P.'s who require special handling. From an employee standpoint, they are usually as welcome in the store as botulism. These V.I.P.'s, many self-appointed, make imperious, and sometimes outrageous demands on the staff. They freely and loudly criticize the service and food preparation, and never bother with anything as déclassé as a tip. *One of the reasons V.I.P.'s are such disruptive elements is that they have very little understanding of the business.* Just knowing the boss confers on them expertise beyond compare.

☑ *B/L Recommends:* For peace and good order, *decide how much special consideration you want shown to your special guests*. We think check signing privileges and the courtesy of cashing personal checks is feasible. You can also supply V.I.P.'s with a password to use to avoid waiting lines during rush hours, but privileges beyond these start to breed more problems than goodwill. Once the prerogatives are determined, you have to firmly and diplomatically pass along the ground rules to your V.I.P. list. They have to be made to understand that in return for special courtesies they are expected to maintain the dress and decorum associated with regular guests. Guest training is in many respects tougher than employee training. That's always the situation when you are dealing with experts.

Those Souper Bowl Prices

One of the classically dumb stunts restaurant execs find hard to resist is the soup cup/bowl gambit. For 90¢, the guests can have a cup of soup, or, they can buy about the same amount in a bowl for almost twice the cost. Anybody that thinks this is smart merchandising has whiffed too much of the dishwashing detergent. This penny con jeopardizes the integrity of the menu and the house itself. If the guests do not spot this kind of friendly rip-off, *be assured one of the waiters or waitresses will tell them about it.*

When the service personnel on the floor do not have confidence in the way menu items are priced, they start handing out hot tips to the guests. This is a fine way to make guests an endangered species: (1) They are chagrined because the serving person has implied they chose a clip joint in which to dine; (2) they mentally start to question the quality and price of everything listed on the menu; (3) they depart the scene vowing never to return.

☑ *B/L Recommends: Honesty is the most profitable policy.* Even the gentlest of menu swindles is capable of backfiring. Most employees resent playing a role in something they regard as vaguely fraudulent. Unless management instructs front end personnel on pricing tactics, employees will misconstrue their intent. These impressions will be relayed one way or another to guests. *Make pricing procedures and sales psychology a regular part of employee meetings.* It will save confusion and keep the guests happy.

Sorry, Our "Special" Is Out to Lunch

Running out of the daily special is no crime. Guests, warned in advance, are disappointed, but usually understand. The real offense is running out of the special and not notifying anyone on the floor. This means waitresses and waiters have to pick tickets up at the windows and double back to the tables. They next have to interest guests in something they don't want. *Guests have requested the special; that is what they want placed on the table.*

The reselling and reordering process takes time. It can cost an entire table turn during the rush hour. Once the turn is lost, it cannot be recovered. Customer relations suffer as well as a result of this kind of amateurism.

☑ *B/L Recommends:* Devise a signaling system so serving personnel know when a special is about to run out. Have serving personnel pull the tabletalkers, menu cards, counter posters, and other merchandisers off the floor as soon as the warning flashes. When the special is depleted, maintain peak sales by having waiters and waitresses suggest comparably priced menu items. *At all costs avoid the loss of time and profits caused by forcing customers to order one meal two times.* Guests have to feel they are getting second-rate treatment when they cannot get what they want the first time they place their orders.

Out of Stock, Out of Business

When customers cannot get what they have ordered, it is a serious problem. The waiter or waitress has to double back and make a resale. The time lost can cost a table turn. The customer is not going to be completely satisfied with his or her second selection and is going to have to wait longer to get it. Out of stock, *the "86" syndrome, is hazardous to any restaurant's profit structure.* Cooks are not always aware of how serious the situation can become. Frequently, they fail to check back-up supplies when going on shift. Others do not like to prepare some items during busy periods. They simply "86" the unit during certain time spans.

☑ *B/L Recommends:* Keep track of "86'd" items. *Have serving personnel mark a meal that cannot be supplied from the galley with an "86" on the guest check.* They will be happy to help out. You are really helping them to do a better customer service job and earn higher tips. Use the "86" findings to determine where the problem is located. Is it in faulty prep work, bad ordering practices? Or has a cook suddenly decided to tell customers what they can or cannot have for lunch?

Dealing With Declining Volume Situations

"What we need is a survey, find out what people really think and want." Every time management attempts to grapple with a declining volume problem, someone comes up with this unbeneficial suggestion right out of college "Marketing I." The most expensive and elaborate customer survey in history produced Ford's Edsel. Anybody in the restaurant business who does not know what customers want should consider another type of career. There are four basic reasons for volume decline: (a) Community economics, (b) Competition, (c) Reduced store visibility, or (d) Internal matters.

There is usually plenty of data available to help pinpoint the source of the problem. You just have to know where to look. The first thing to do is determine the date when volume slippage became apparent. Next, effect a match up of that time and the above listed possibilities. If community economics are the problem, this can be readily determined by checking with the local bank, nearby realtors, retailers, and the chamber of commerce. If competition is the culprit which it seldom is for a well run operation, a fast visit to the local newspaper office will give some indication. Check back issues just before and just after the volume slippage date. How much new restaurant advertising is shown? Changes in street traffic patterns, or newly erected buildings can reduce store visibility and influence volume. A ten-minute drive around the area in the morning and evening rush periods will provide an answer on the question of visibility. *Internal matters, item (D), deserve close study.* Which employees were brought into the operation shortly before the slippage started? What menu changes were instituted?

What directives and instructions were issued to the staff?

☑ *B/L Recommends:* Always start your research with item (D), internal matters. Most of the time this is the source of the problem. *Happily, it also is the place where corrections are easiest to make.* Once in a while, some combination of the four factors may be in evidence. As restaurant consultants, we once worked on one such situation. It involved a full service operation that had been in the community for years. Volume suddenly went into a nosedive. What we found was a store manager so intimidated by the opening of a nearby shopping mall with many food outlets that he let his own restaurant go to ruin. He also convinced the absentee owners of the store there was little hope for the future. *What he was doing was actually forcing customers to go someplace else to dine.* When the problem was cleared up, store volume climbed immediately. The shopping center was attracting more people to the area and the store started reaping the benefits. If competition had been accepted as the chief reason for the volume slump, a serious situation could have been compounded into a catastrophe.

Economics, competition, and store visibility are factors that are usually quite apparent. Not so with internal matters. These items are usually camouflaged by prejudice, lack of knowledge, and sometimes outright stupidity.

As we have stressed elsewhere, it is very important that every document used in store administration carry a date. When things start to go wrong, that's the place to start looking for reasons. Customer surveys can produce Edsels, internal surveys generally come up with results.

Scratchy Sounds Can Tear Up Ambiance

In-house music systems are now as standard as cash registers in a store. Hour after hour they hum their tunes softly complementing the restaurant's ambiance. Very little maintenance is necessary, therefore very little management attention is directed to this area. Unfortunately, the quality of the sound starts to deteriorate the day the system is turned on. When an irritating scratchy sound starts coming over the system, *most of the time it is caused by deterioration of the glue which holds speaker cones in place.* Some guests are highly sensitive to this form of annoyance.

☑ *B/L Recommends:* It takes a conscious effort to check the in-house music system. Managers get so used to constant background music in the front end that they become immune to whatever the speakers are putting out. Not so the guests. *Inferior sound quality requires immediate attention.*

Common Sense Is Not a Common Commodity

There is little danger of Harvey, the manager, ever losing his head. Nobody would want to take it. If a busboy slipped and broke his arm, Harvey would demand the kid clock out with his good hand before going to the hospital. If there were a blaze in the dining room, he'd ask firefighters to leave those messy hoses outside. The Harveys in restaurant management contribute a lot—*mainly to the hidden costs of running a store.*

In response to a client request, we recently toured a full service operation managed by a Harvey-type. It took place during a heavy noon rush. Harvey's eagle-like gaze swept the dining room. Then he directed the hostess to immediately reprimand one waitress for improper uniform, another for not holding a water glass in the approved manner, and a third for not having her apron strings tied in the proper bow. He could not have disrupted the work flow on the floor better if he had dug a ditch from the cashstand to the pass bar. But he showed everybody who was the boss. These displays of managerial immaturity cost money.

☑ **B/L Recommends:** Insist that managers exhibit signs of judgment and leadership before awarding them the title. *Knowledge of company regulations alone is not sufficient qualification.* Blasting personnel while they are under peak pressure is dumb. A smart manager knows when to relieve the pressure with compliments, not complaints; with assistance, not high-handed superiority. The time for preventive action is ahead of the rush hour. The time for corrective action is after the rush hour.

Quickie Business Surveys

Who is doing the most business in town? When the answer to this question has to be learned in a hurry, parking lot checks and traffic counts are not the most reliable sources. There is a fast, fairly accurate way to acquire this information.

☑ **B/L Recommends:** *Count the number of newspaper racks* in front of the eating places. A lot of racks indicates high customer activity on the premises. Newspaper distributors do not waste their racks or papers on places where the sales are slow.

Getting a Meeting into the Right Rut

If you need time to doze off at a management operations conference, wait until a topic is introduced—anything will do, a food suggestion, or a service item is just fine. Quickly get the floor and say, "We could do it like _____," (fill the blank with the name of a competing chain that is larger than your own). *That statement stops a meeting faster than disc brakes.* It's good for a pleasant snooze while everybody narrows their thinking to what the competitor is allegedly doing so successfully. Not only that, the statement is a standard feature of most operations management conferences. Your colleagues will be grateful for getting the affair off in the right rut. Don't be afraid to join in on this brainstorming on what the competitor is doing—that's what keeps our industry so imitative. Other than wasting some time, the words are pretty harmless. A person or a committee will be assigned to look into the matter in question and report back later. That's good for more rest time at a subsequent date.

☑ **B/L Recommends:** *Keep references to the competition out of your management meetings.* Insist that topics be studied within the framework of your own organization. What the competition is doing may or may not be right for you. One thing is sure, they have been doing it far longer than your group. It's tough to make a profit playing catch-up ball.

Planning Can Cut Remodeling Costs

There comes a time in the life of every store when it has to be remodeled or renovated. It is a big ticket item. In many instances, *extra expense is generated through inadequate prior planning.* Remodeling is a complex operation. The temptation to turn the task over to the contractor that promises the lowest cost and least down time is very strong. That's where a lot of trouble starts.

☑ **B/L Recommends:** *Select your prime contractor with exceeding care.* The completion provisions in a contract are all very necessary. However, you want a remodeling job done; acquiring ammunition for a lawsuit is not the real objective. This means you need a contractor that has a proven performance record working with the restaurants in your local area. Ask all the potential bidders for your job for references. You should personally check out each reference supplied.

The next thing to do is write down everything that has to be done. Be detailed and specific. You will want to use the list in preparing bid solicitations and also as a subsequent checklist to be sure the work was finished correctly. Go over the list with your bidders to determine how much work can be done in advance off the premises, then quickly moved into position during the shutdown period. From the minute you close for renovations, *you are fighting the clock to get open again.* To do it right, you need a contractor that is an ally, not an amateur.

Picasso

When Pablo Picasso placed anything on paper it immediately became a painting of tremendous value. It did not matter what medium he worked in: watercolor, oil, pencil, pen: They all sold. His ability to transmit ideas on paper or canvas made him a master in his own time. There is only one Picasso. The majority of us cannot even write our signatures legibly, and certainly art is not our occupation. So why is it that we hand-print signs in a crude attempt to communicate items of importance to people?

☑ **B/L Recommends:** Hand-painted and grease-penciled signs usually look terrible! Amateurish signs with uneven writing and lettering can seriously cheapen your total concept. Your employees will not take pride if you do not. Your customers will not appreciate being asked to purchase something that has the appearance of being of poor quality.

Fifty Percent Is a Bad Average

There's a strong possibility that a full restaurant only has a 50-percent occupancy at the peak of the rush hour. When many restaurants were designed, four-place tops got priority locations. The reasoning was based on the characteristics of the American family. In the 50's and early 60's, family units averaged out to three persons or more, and the number was on an upward trend. Then zero population growth came along to turn the pattern around. The result is that a lot of dining rooms are not as efficient as they once were. The fastest way to check on this factor is by surveying the parking lot during a rush period against the number of seats occupied inside. If the parking lot is filled, but there are unoccupied seats at many four-place tops, the turnover factor is not all it should be.

☑ *B/L Recommends:* If you think turnover can be improved during rush periods, establish a guest check audit to get the facts. Figure out how much those unoccupied seats at four-place tops are costing you. The figure can be significant. More emphasis on deuce seating can provide the privacy guests want, and the improved turnover you need.

Don't Exterminate the Guests

Some exterminator services bug us. Their trucks and uniforms stridently proclaim they are out to rid the earth of all bugs and infestations. They operate on the premise that being highly visible increases their business. That's fine, but only if it doesn't reduce yours. Most restaurant guests are aware of the need for exterminator services. They use them for their homes and offices. *Guests just hate to face that fact.* They don't like to dwell on the thought of dining at infested premises. When a garishly decorated exterminator's truck is parked close to the front door and a uniformed attendant unloads equipment, it is automatically assumed the restaurant is having a big bug problem.

☑ *B/L Recommends:* Insist that your bug killers operate on a low profile basis. Most owners of these services are familiar with the unique problems restaurants have in this regard. However, this does not apply to their route representatives. They'll bust through the front door at high noon and start spraying away at the critters. Instead, the trucks should be parked in the most unobtrusive area available. The representative should enter the premises through the back door, and the work should only be accomplished during designated low volume periods. Also, find out what effect the toxicants will have on the bugs and vermin. Some sprays force bugs to surface from cracks, crevices, and drains. This has advantages only if you can remove the carcasses before your guests happen to see them. *Keep in mind that you are paying the exterminator to get rid of bugs, not guests.*

Fussing on the Phone Solves Nothing

You could bathe a hippo in the parking lot pothole. Customer cars have been damaged both by hitting the hole and trying to avoid it. The shopping center management says they'll take care of it. *At least that's what they promised last year.* The restaurant's owner says he has called several times since about the problem, but can't get action. We showed him how to do it with a postage stamp.

☑ *B/L Recommends:* When the second telephone call fails to get results, *put everything in writing.* Do not be Mr. or Mrs. Nice Guy either. Clearly state the danger that exists, the estimated loss in business per day while the condition exists, and what you want done. *Note at the end of the letter who is receiving copies:* your legal counsel, any civil authority that might have jurisdiction, and the major retailer in the center should all receive copies. That way, the person to whom your letter is addressed will logically conclude you are considering legal action if things are not fixed in a hurry. Fruitless telephone calls in these situations are a waste of everybody's time.

Cut the Numbers—Who Needs Customers?

The unit Harry manages is part of a city-wide chain. In his managerial capacity, *Harry reneges on an average of 80 "contracts" a day.* You would think this would upset the home office. It might, if they knew about it. However, Harry is something of a company celebrity so nobody snoops around his operation. Every month, Harry posts the best food-cost percentage in the entire organization. This is a difficult feat. The company has been doing a lot of experimenting with new menu items. The artificially set food-cost percentage goal has not been adjusted for some time. *The way Harry has attained his star status is by simply not serving certain things promised on the menu.* His unique approach to "cutting the numbers" is shooting holes in the company's menu research project. But with Harry's company, results count first and foremost.

☑ *B/L Recommends:* A menu should be regarded as a contract between the customer and the restaurant. The menu promises certain products and services in exchange for a clearly stated price. *Delivering less is a violation of that contract.* A foodservice organization that fails to get this important point across to managers is going to get in trouble.

For Restaurants in Red-Light Districts

While it may not be your fault, some of the bad feelings are going to rub off if customers receive parking tickets while on your premises. It's bad enough to be blamed for the things you do without having to take the blame for the mistakes of others.

☑ *B/L Recommends:* Restaurants located in heavy traffic areas *where parking regulations are strictly enforced, can be heroes by posting a notice to that effect.* It can be on the entrance, next to the register, or on a table tent. Care about your customers so they can care for you.

Rate Your Competitor

We've heard operators speak tolerantly of their competitors with such statements as, *"He's really no competition."* We wonder.

☑ *B/L Recommends:* Normal people eat only one lunch a day. If they eat it at some other restaurant, they won't eat it at your place. That's what competition does. Go to your competitor. Order something he or she does well. Evaluate the result, then *return to your restaurant and do it better.* That's when the other guy is "no competition."

Audit-Oddities

Is cost accounting a mystery to you? Does record-keeping frighten you? Do you leave such important information to the judgment of your accountant? Is it possible that whoever does your books is not aware of such things as yields, net purchases, frequency of sale, missing guest checks, waste, pilferage, non-ring ups, fast and slow sellers, substitutions, pricing, and menu planning? Merely subtracting opening inventories from ending inventories is not enough to really zero in on food costs and usage. The ticket, computer or guest check system you use to order and obtain foods from your kitchen can supply amazing information when you perform your own in-house "guest check audit."

We know of one chain that produced over 2,000 cups of coffee in one week, which they thought they had sold to their customers. The owners, who were in business to make money, found their waitresses simply neglected to write guest checks properly and/or ring them up on the cash register, as they pocketed the coffee and tax money as "tips." The guest check audit that was introduced for the very first time, turned things around, proving the value of using a pre-printed guest check with a numerical sequence to avoid missing foods, money, and checks.

☑ *B/L Recommends:* Isolate a week in the life of your foodservice establishment. Take a beginning and ending inventory for the period. Note the total sales. Collect every guest check, and account for those that are missing, if possible. Hire some dependable high school youngsters to make a master list of every item, variation, and substitution that can be served in your operation. List the number of times each item was served. Just taking the process this far will produce illuminating evidence. Some items will post greater sales records than you believed was the case, while others may show such slow sales that you may wish to discontinue them when planning your next menu. Next, analyze each group to determine the quantity (yield) that should have been consumed, comparing the reported sales to the net differences (purchases) between your beginning and ending inventories. Discrepancies will surface, revealing waste and pilferage. You might also find some meals were "sold" but never rung up on your register.

Once you have tied the audit package together, let your crew know your findings and analysis. You will gain their respect. Improvements in virtually every area will be immediate.

Police Your Banquet

Meetings, banquets, parties, weddings, testimonials, and the like have a double effect on your business. First, you profit from a banquet itself, and, *second, you profit from the exposure to people who might never have come into your restaurant.* Some details can be a problem, however. There may be a sudden demand on your parking facilities. This may force banquet guests to park at some distance from your lot. Drunks, hoodlums, and panhandlers can ruin what might have been a positive experience.

☑ ***B/L Recommends:*** *Include the police in your planning.* When banquet orders are made up, send one to the kitchen, one to accounting, one to the banquet manager, and one to the police. They can patrol your street in greater force when guests are either arriving or departing.

For the private use of foodservice employees who wish to communicate with their owners and managers:

"THINGS I WANT TO SAY"

Dear Boss: Yes, there are certain things I want to suggest that concern our establishment, employees, and customers. I do have definite opinions and ideas that may have a constructive effect on the things we do.

(Note: Please read the questionnaire *before* giving any answers. Mark "N.A." if item is not applicable to your shift or responsibilities. You do not have to mention others by name or sign your own name if you do not care to do so. Please return this questionnaire as soon as possible so that constructive action can be taken to improve everything that we are doing.)

1. **Menu and Prices.** I recommend we add, change, or eliminate the following; my reasons are:
   a) Breakfast _____

   b) Lunch _____

   c) Dinner _____

   d) Sandwiches _____

   e) Soups & Salads _____

   f) Appetizers & Side Orders _____

g) House Specialties_____

h) Desserts & Baked Items _____

i) Beverages _____

j) Take-Out Items & Supplies _____

k) Catering, Banquets, & Room Service _____

l) Other Foods & Beverages _____

m) I have these comments to offer concerning our plastics, paper, chinaware, silverware, and glassware (i.e.: supply, quality, sizes, convenience) _____

2. I believe the *worst item* we serve is (and why): _____
_____

3. I believe the *finest item* we serve is (and why): _____
_____

4. I believe the *worst thing* we do to our customers is (explain): ____
_____

5. I believe we are *best known* to our customers for the following reasons (explain): _____

6. I believe we *have too much wastage of food* and other restaurant supplies in our preparation, kitchen, counter, and front areas that can be reduced, or eliminated (explain): _____
_____

7. *Safety* is important for the well being of everyone. I think we can improve in these areas (explain): _____
    _____

8. *Cleanliness and sanitation* is everyone's responsibility. I think we can improve in these areas, stations, and duties (explain): _____
    _____

9. *Security* is very important. I recommend that we can save money, avoid holdups, and reduce the loss of cash, foods, and supplies that we as employees are responsible for (explain): _____
    _____

10. I believe we can *save energy* (gas, oil, water, electricity etc.) if we do the following: _____
    _____

11. *Teamwork and cooperation* between all employees and management personnel are of the greatest importance. I believe we can improve in many areas such as: gossiping, hurting each other, doing less than fair share of work, etc. (explain): _____
    _____

12. I believe we are not consistent with our *food and beverage substitutions* on my shift and between our various meal shifts. The following is my list of things that I understand that I am allowed to substitute at no charge, or for a price:

    SUBSTITUTION LIST

Regular Menu Item	Substitute For	No Charge	Charge

13. And, last but not least, I wish to offer these final suggestions, compliments and complaints in an effort to help everyone to enjoy our working conditions and relationship with each other so that our establishment can be the best place in which to work or eat: _____
    _____

I have been in the foodservice industry in one capacity or another for _____ years. The ideas and suggestions that I have given are based upon my own personal and professional experience. I hope they will be used to correct and improve our business. Thank you for asking for my opinions.

Sincerely,

Unit # _____
Establishment: _____   _____

All Is Not Lost When a P.R. Message Gets Across

Part of good customer service is looking after the customer's property when it gets mislaid. *This is an area where restaurants can rack up many public relations points,* yet few take advantage of the opportunity. Eyeglasses, lighters, and key chains get dumped into a large box. When somebody phones to inquire about a missing item, whoever takes the call has to paw through a bunch of dust and junk accumulated over a long period of time. It is a distasteful, time-wasting task. When a lost item is located, it is usually restored to the owner without appropriate comment or flourish.

☑ *B/L Recommends:* Have pouch-type envelopes and tags printed. The envelopes are for small items, the tags for umbrellas, coats, and packages. When an employee finds a stray item, he or she simply fills in the blanks in the printed message:

(Name of restaurant) is happy to return your (item description). It was found by (name of employee) in the (location—dining room, parking lot, etc.) on (date and time).

Listing the time and date makes the handling of phone inquiries fast and simple. It also makes the management of the lost and found box a great deal easier.

When lost property is restored with this kind of information attached, the owner usually realizes that a gratuity or reward is in order. This encourages employees to turn in stray articles, instead of appropriating them for their own use.

Melt the Ice

Virtually every foodservice operator fears that something made of glass will break into or near the ice bin. We all fear that our customers will get cut and sue us for negligence.

☑ *B/L Recommends:* Issue strict instructions to everyone that should any glass or other item be broken in or near your ice, the complete ice bin must be washed down with hot water. It is important to melt all the ice so glass particles can be safely and completely removed. Inexperienced help afraid of a reprimand will keep it a secret that they broke things near or into the ice bin. They will try to pick out the clear particles of glass or plastic and think they have removed all of them. This can be very dangerous!

Does the Cook Have Experience Under Fire?

The cook claimed he was experienced. His experience apparently did not include combatting a fat fire. When the fat flared, our hero hit it with a handy pan of water. That ended the day's business for the store.

☑ *B/L Recommends:* Find out what your cooks know about fire fighting. Keep a package of baking soda handy in the galley. Show cooks how efficiently it shuts down a pan fire.

The Four-Minute Calamity

It took four minutes to wipe out the family business. It was a fried chicken franchise. Like other members of the chain, the owners employed young, unskilled help. According to the company representative, this was supposed to be profitable. When the deep fryer caught fire there was only one counter attendant in the store. *Nobody had told her how to use the fire extinguisher.* She panicked after the bowl of water she threw at the flames spread the fire across the walls of the galley. The fire department managed to save the neighboring real estate office.

☑ *B/L Recommends: Obviously, fire fighting drills and instructions are important.* What owners and managers fail to appreciate is that the first fire is always the worst. Everyone believes it cannot happen; no one is really prepared.

Warning Tracks—Big League Safety Item

When the baseball franchise installed warning tracks next to the outfield walls there was an impressive reduction in the injury rate among players. This is a lesson that should be applied in the restaurant game as well.

☑ *B/L Recommends:* Create a distinct change in the floor texture in front of dangerous swinging doors. *Change carpeted surfaces to hard surfaces three yards in front of the doors.* Look for scuff marks and wall scratches in other areas. They indicate places where personnel are bumping into obstacles. Install your own warning track system at these locations. Keep injuries from benching your team members.

Talk Radio

Radio and television programs have turned to straight talk shows and interviews to increase their share of the listening audience. The radio and TV celebrities cover almost every subject, and are most interesting. They can succeed in getting people to forget about their work and troubles. However, there is one big problem: *What if the people who are trying to forget about their work happen to be at work? What if the people are your cooks and service personnel?* Radios and even television sets are all too often to be found in prep kitchens, galleys, and service stations. We are not referring to the equipment that is usually available for guests in bars, lounges, and waiting areas.

☑ *B/L Recommends:* Radios and TV sets in your employee work stations should be "86"ed. They are a definite distraction. They are often the reason why cooks, for example, do not hear the food orders given them by your waiters and waitresses. Employees using mixers, knives, and slicing machines must keep their minds on what they are doing.

We convinced one manager in a fast food unit to get rid of the radios in his prep area. His counter people were accident prone; there were six sliced finger accidents in one month. We posted a sign: *"Do not talk when using slicer."* There have been fewer mishaps.

Professionals do not listen to radio or watch TV during their shifts. Amateurs will test you. They know they are wrong. They want to see if you know they are out of line and intend to do something about it. It is a playful test, yet one you must pass if you are to keep control of your business.

Dumpsters Seldom Tell Lies

Something that can tell your future more accurately than a fortune cookie is the dumpster outside the back door. Observant sanitarians usually check the condition and contents of the dumpster before they go into a store. A dirty, grease-streaked dumpster gets these official visits off to a very poor start. Empty margarine containers in the dumpster when your menu guarantees everything cooked in butter is almost a sure sign that your future is going to be clouded with unpleasantness from the health department. *Customers who have to park in the back lot also see the dumpster.* When it is messy and smelly, there's not much hope for greater profits in the future.

☑ *B/L Recommends:* Look at your dumpster. If it is in bad shape, call the service and have it replaced with a new unit. After that, keep it clean, as you would any other part of the restaurant. The exterior should get a wash down after emptying. It should be turned on its side and the inside hosed out over a drain. *Ideally, after the trash is checked, put it in sealed plastic bags,* and then into the dumpster. Your future will be blessed with friendly neighbors, customers, and an occasional sanitarian.

Gripes Need Top Level Attention

Handling customer gripes is as much fun as a trip to the dentist. We notice more and more managers delegating this onerous chore to waiters and waitresses. It is a mistake. When serving personnel are given the okay to make good on complaints, a lot of guests start enjoying meals on the house. Worse, *very few miscues get the right corrective attention.* In some respects gripes work like emergency alarms; that's why the manager has to stay alert to them. It may not be just that one order of scallops that "tastes funny," all ten pounds could be bad.

☑ *B/L Recommends:* Only a manager should decide what kind of attention a gripe requires and whether it is valid or not. Serving personnel give top priority to protecting their tips. When they handle gripes their emphasis is on smoothing over the effect, not correcting the cause.

Stoop Policy

Trade papers frequently report the great things our industry's leaders have accomplished. Many are credited with being fine chefs, great designers, excellent leaders, creative idea people, and financial wizards. Most of us only know these operators by what we read or hear. Few of us ever have the opportunity to see these people in action, under pressure, at their own work. We have also known other executives who were singularly brilliant in certain ways but, as the records show, less than adequate in others. What is it that makes people great?

☑ *B/L Recommends:* We believe it is the little things that make people great. Regardless of the uniqueness of our businesses, it takes people to operate them and good leaders to motivate their personnel. Saying hello, remembering names, giving compliments, and really caring about his or her people are personality traits that denote a great person.

We particularly admire, for example, managers who follow their own "stoop policy." They set the example. Whenever they see a piece of paper, a mess, or an improper item on the floor, they stoop over and pick it up. They know that if they can do it their people will see them and follow their example. Those who practice what they preach are to be respected and congratulated. We can predict that these people are, or will become in the future, our leaders. *Good managers are never too good to stoop.*

Here, I'll Get the Tab

How nice it is to dine out, especially when the other person picks up our meal check. Somehow a dinner tastes better when the price is right.

We in our restaurants are quite used to eating for nothing. After all, it is a necessity. The whole place is our responsibility, and with it comes a few fringe benefits, not the least being that our meals are on the house. But what of those guests, family members, friends, and sales reps who visit our establishments? A free cup of coffee is one thing, but a meal is our business. *Most of us cannot afford to give away any business.*

If we operated a ready-to-wear store our friends would certainly expect to pay for what they want to take with them. One thing is for sure—no one would expect to get their clothing for nothing. But with food it is different. Some people expect us to pick up their guest checks just because we talk to them, sit with them, or purchase merchandise from them. We're all familiar with the situation. Some of us have set up defenses to avoid picking up tabs. We have known owners who refused to work their dining rooms for fear of being placed in the uncomfortable position of having to pick up tabs or refuse to pay for people. Our waiters and waitresses do not help us either, as they *assume* that certain people are our guests and, therefore, neglect to present a guest check. Then comes the embarrassing moment when the guests get up to leave. Who's to pay?

☑ *B/L Recommends:* Be strict. Insist that every customer receive a guest check according to a sound system of procedures. If your operation calls for the check to be delivered at the end of the meal—so be it. If the check is to be given with the delivery of the entree—do it! If the order is to be paid and collected before its delivery, again, be sure that everyone follows your rules. The safest and most positive way to avoid embarrassment and the loss of gross sales is to be sure your guests receive their tab at the proper moment. Then, if you want to pick it up you can, with the appropriate flourish and comment. If not, you can discreetly get up and move on about your business. Your meaning is clear. Do not allow your personnel to make *your* decision for you.

It's What's Up Front That Counts

The majority of us have a great tendency to blame our cooks and back-of-the-house personnel for waste, oversized portions, and lack of controls that result in higher food costs. We count our steaks, meats, and other expensive items in our attempts to control our cost-of-sales. We tighten our inventories and double check our systems to see that waiters, waitresses, and counter personnel do not take any food from kitchen areas without a properly completed form or guest check. We want to get paid for everything we buy or produce. We show our concern for everything in the rear, but unfortunately forget about what is *right before our eyes*.

☑ *B/L Recommends:* Concentrate your attention on those numerous costly fruits, juices, dessert items, and other foods and beverages that are always available to your service personnel in front of your kitchen and galley areas and do not need to be requisitioned by a written or oral order. Waiters and waitresses who want to be liked by their customers know their tips will be greater if they can give away little goodies without charge. Toast, extra butter, salads, tomatoes, dressings, breads, rolls, pies, cakes, beer, wine, appetizers, soups, coffee, tea, milk, and soft drinks that you have placed up front for "convenience" can run up your food costs several points. And these are percentages you may never be able to locate.

Service personnel like to con bosses and managers into thinking that they are great workers, that they follow standard operating procedures, and that they can work better and faster if certain items are made available to them out front. Do not believe them!

Place out front only those items that must be there. Keep all you can inside your kitchen areas, making it necessary for your people to involve another person in each transaction. Check to determine if you are receiving a good return on your investment in foodstuffs that are located on the "honor" side of the counter.

Service personnel do not realize that the waste or give-away of one slice of pie wipes out the profit on the whole pie. Few appreciate that a simple glass of milk may well be one of your highest food cost items. Remember, what's up front does count a great deal.

Tracking Kitchen Performance

Once the waiter or waitress has made the sale, how does the good manager keep track of the various stages of preparation that make up a meal? It's obvious when the tables are watered, get coffee or other beverages, and when soups or salads have been delivered. *But where does kitchen production stand?* There are checks on the wheel, but when will they be up?

☑ *B/L Recommends:* One manager we met had a simple solution (all great ideas are basically simple). The waiter or waitress placed the check on the wheel upside down. The cook turned it right side up to read it. "Right side up" checks were "working." Upside down checks weren't. The manager always knew when he should offer to go into the kitchen to lend a hand.

A Sense of Humor Can Go a Long Way

How many of us exhibit dual personalities? Are we serious, definite, and forceful at work and easy going pussycats at home? Are we the life of the party socially, and tyrants in our business?

We have seen dozens of owners and managers treat their customers (wisely) with great charm and humor, but the employees with temperamental outbursts and bitterness (unwisely). Some of us have learned to mix a sense of humor with the serious aspects of our operations. Can't we relax a bit to enjoy ourselves, our guests, and our personnel—and let them enjoy being with us?

☑ *B/L Recommends:* For openers, take a good look at your printed forms. You have everything to gain if you can psychologically loosen up those who have to use them. Add a touch of humor. For example, we created this guest receipt for one chain:

Dear Boss: I just had a great meal. I only spent $_____ on <u>(date)</u>_____.
Important business was discussed with _____. It was worth every penny of it.

Signed, Your loyal employee _____

P.S. To the I.R.S.: This was a perfectly deductible business expense. You too should eat here when in the neighborhood.

Try a bit of humor with the form that you use to record cash register overrings to let you reconcile your tape totals with your cash.

Date _____   Restaurant#_____

Dear Boss: I just made an overring on our register.

       I actually recorded: $_____.

       It should have been: $_____.

       The difference is: $_____which means our cash will not balance without this note. I have attached the guest check and have left it with this form under the cash tray so you can balance our tape reading with our actual cash. I'll try to be more careful.

Your favorite cashier _____.

You can get your point across when you use words with a built-in smile.

APPENDIX

-

*The woodpecker owes his success
to the fact that he uses his head
and keeps pecking away
until he finishes the job.*

APPENDIX

EMPLOYMENT AGREEMENT

This agreement is made and entered into between   , hereinafter referred to as "Employer," and   , hereinafter referred to as "Employee."

Whereas, employer has created a unique plan for the establishment of a specialized foodservice operation and is at present engaged in improving techniques and promotions for the sales of its products and services under registered trademarks known as   ,

Whereas, employer, to enhance its value, has created methods and systems which include, among other things, design of building, layout of equipment, operating methods, menus of special design, pricing psychology, advertising, sales techniques, signs, interior and exterior decor, uniforms, personnel management, training, recordkeeping, customized serviceware, and controls, all of which are referred to as "The System,"

Whereas, employer has invested thousands, even millions, of dollars in such development, has given personal guarantee and taken personal risks to open one or more restaurants,

Whereas, employer desires to hire employee and employee desires to accept such employment under the terms and conditions contained in this agreement. It is understood that employee solicited employer for the job-position and did agree to fulfill the stipulated duties with a cooperative attitude when hired.

Now, therefore, employer recognizes that employee has much to learn and shall not charge employee any fees, money, or require payment of any kind for the instruction and teaching of a trade, but shall pay to employee a wage or salary at no less than the prevailing minimum wage for work performed as specified.

Grant. Employer hereby grants to employee the right to work at this one location and not to be transferred without the employee's specific approval. However, employee agrees not to withhold such permission when it is clearly understood that such services are needed.

Exclusive. Employer shall not appoint or allow another employee to perform such duties within the territory specified as employee's work area providing employee shall faithfully perform them.

Term. The term of this agreement shall be forever unless sooner terminated by either party.

Nature of grant. Employer agrees to divulge to employee all its special secrets, recipes, methods, systems, and controls through initial orientation, consistent education, communication, testing, and on-the-job instruction. Furthermore, employee shall have access to many parts of the restaurant including, at times, cash and valuable food and equipment. It is expressly agreed that ownership of all processes, systems, recipes, and materials is and shall remain vested solely in employer, and employee agrees to keep everything in complete confidence hereunder.

Services of employer

Premises & supplies. Employer agrees to construct the building, pay all leasehold improvements, equip the restaurant, and purchase and stock it with sufficient inventory of foodstuffs to be able to operate it at maximum efficiency.

Advertising. Employer shall develop advertising, public relations, and promotional campaigns, and shall expend such sums of money as may be needed to attract customers and shall bear the cost of any price reductions or other customer inducements that it may elect to use to maintain and increase customer count, volume, and profits. Employee shall not pay anything.

Training & supervision. Employer agrees to train employee in all duties of the restaurant with such theory and practical on-the-job instruction as may be required. Employer reserves the right to supervise the employee to determine if there has been any breach of this agreement.

Confidential manuals. Employer agrees to furnish sections of its confidential manual of operations and employee agrees to maintain its confidentiality.

Payments to employee. Employer agrees to pay promptly at each scheduled pay period the appropriate hourly wage, less authorized deductions. It is understood that all pay increases are to be earned on merit, with the exception of all annual increases as required by state and federal minimum wage regulations. Employee is not required, by law, to improve in expertise, performance, attitude, or intelligence but only to be present and an employee in good standing to receive such automatic wage increases.

Fringe benefits. Employer agrees to pay for certain other benefits such as workmen's compensation and insurance as may be required under local, state, and federal laws, thereby increasing the actual wages paid by an amount ranging from 10 percent to over 20 percent. Employer agrees to provide uniforms so that employees will not incur excess wear and tear on their personal clothing. Employer shall supply certain menu items free of charge or at minimum cost to properly feed employees, as an additional saving to them.

It is further agreed that employees who earn tips shall keep all extra monies, often ranging from several dollars to many thousands of dollars—all produced because of the employer's creation of a pleasant atmosphere and conditions that are conducive to the giving of gratuities by guests.

Tipped employees shall make no investment in their work stations or other materials to earn such extra income. Employees are required only to contribute good attitude and teamwork, and possibly small sums of money to certain service personnel for their assistance in accordance with any unwritten policies of the restaurant or locality.

Duties of employee

The system. Employee agrees that every detail of the system is most important and must be complied with at all times, including, but not limited to, uniformity, quality, service, customer comfort, portion control, cleanliness, and prevention of waste and pilferage.

Fixtures & equipment. Employee agrees to maintain all such items in good working condition in accordance with employer's standard operating procedures.

Foods. Employee agrees not to waste, destroy, or otherwise misuse the foods, beverages, or supplies of the employer. Employee agrees not to steal, pilfer, or otherwise cause employer to lose anything of value.

Scheduled hours. Employee agrees to fulfill his or her job obligations, at all times, as scheduled and without complaint. Employee agrees to advise employer of all changes of address or telephone. Employee agrees to advise employer of expected tardiness or absence with sufficient notice so that a suitable replacement can be located. If one cannot be found, then employee shall protect employer by performing such duties, as scheduled.

Recordkeeping & gross sales. Employee agrees to add, subtract, multiply, and extend all figures correctly and to maintain all guest checks, cash register tapes, and related information in accurate form.

All monies accepted from customers, as gross sales, are to be handled correctly and maintained in locked and safe conditions at all times, with no alterations, falsifications, other misinformation, or loss.

Security. Employee agrees to protect employer and its property by the prompt and accurate disclosure of those who would endanger its success by pilferage, breakage, waste, theft, or removal of property, money, or foodstuffs, or by willful negligence.

Standard operating procedures. Employee agrees to abide by all rules displayed or available to all employees, that employer has proven to be desirable for the successful operation of its restaurant through years of experience, research, and development. Employee, furthermore, agrees to faithfully and strictly abide by all standard operating procedures and not change them without first obtaining permission from employer.

Remedies for breach-termination. Employee acknowledges that strict performance of all the terms and conditions of this agreement is necessary and that employer will give prompt written "warning notice" to all who willfully disobey such conditions. Employee shall cure such defaults immediately and, without repetition, continuously perform his or her duties in an acceptable manner. Continued disobedience will result in termination and all such actions will be properly documented in employee's personal file.

It is expressly understood that falsification of any information, stealing, willful negligence, customer discourtesy, use of alcohol or drugs on the premises, or behavior on duty under their influence, willful disobedience, or insubordination will result in immediate termination with no opportunity for re-hire. Employer, as a result of employee's unacceptable performance, as stated, shall be under no obligation to give any positive references to potential employers of employee.

Bankruptcy. Employee realizes that should he or she be unfaithful to this agreement that employer may lose money and face the possibility of bankruptcy, in which case said employee and all other employees will lose their jobs, wages, fringe benefits, tips, and other advantages.

Notices. Employee agrees, with the signing of this agreement, that he or she will give proper notice of intention to terminate employment so that employer may have sufficient opportunity to secure a qualified replacement.

Employee agrees to return all uniforms and other materials that belong to the employer in good condition, with the exception of the valuable experience that employee has gained—free of charge—while in the employment of employer.

Arbitration. Both parties agree to hold open and friendly discussions at all times during the term of this agreement to settle all grievances and misunderstandings, but also agree that they will at no time openly argue or discuss such grievances in front of any guests or other employees.

It is understood that this agreement is not 100 percent valid or enforceable in a court of law, but is, as agreed, a reasonable and fair understanding of the respective duties and responsibilities of the employer and employee.

In Witness Whereof, the parties have executed this agreement this
of   , 19
Employer   Employee
By

"A Model Employment Agreement" by Leon Gottlieb first appeared in the March 1, 1978 issue of *Restaurant Business Magazine,* copyright 1978, Bill Communications, Inc.